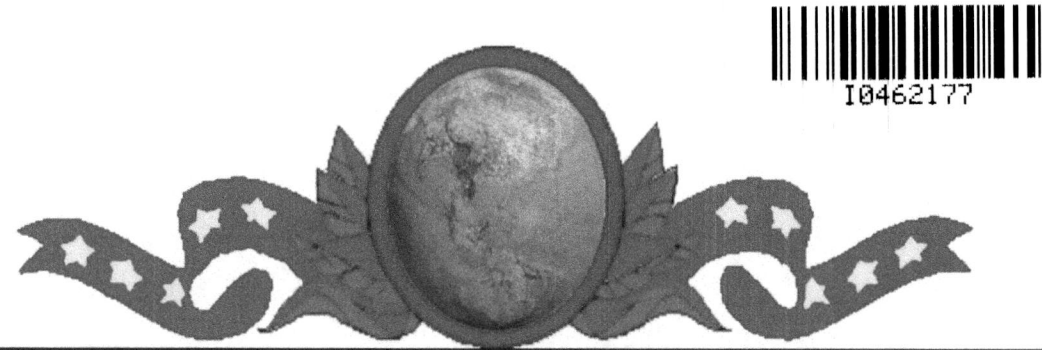

Real World
Colouring Book
For Advanced Users & Adults

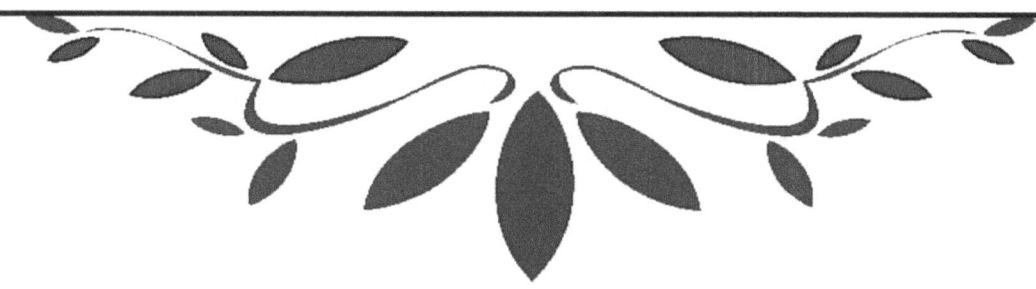

Copyright 2019 By John Boom

50 Images

Created From Real Life Photos
For You To Colour As You Please.

ISBN 978-0-359-78780-7

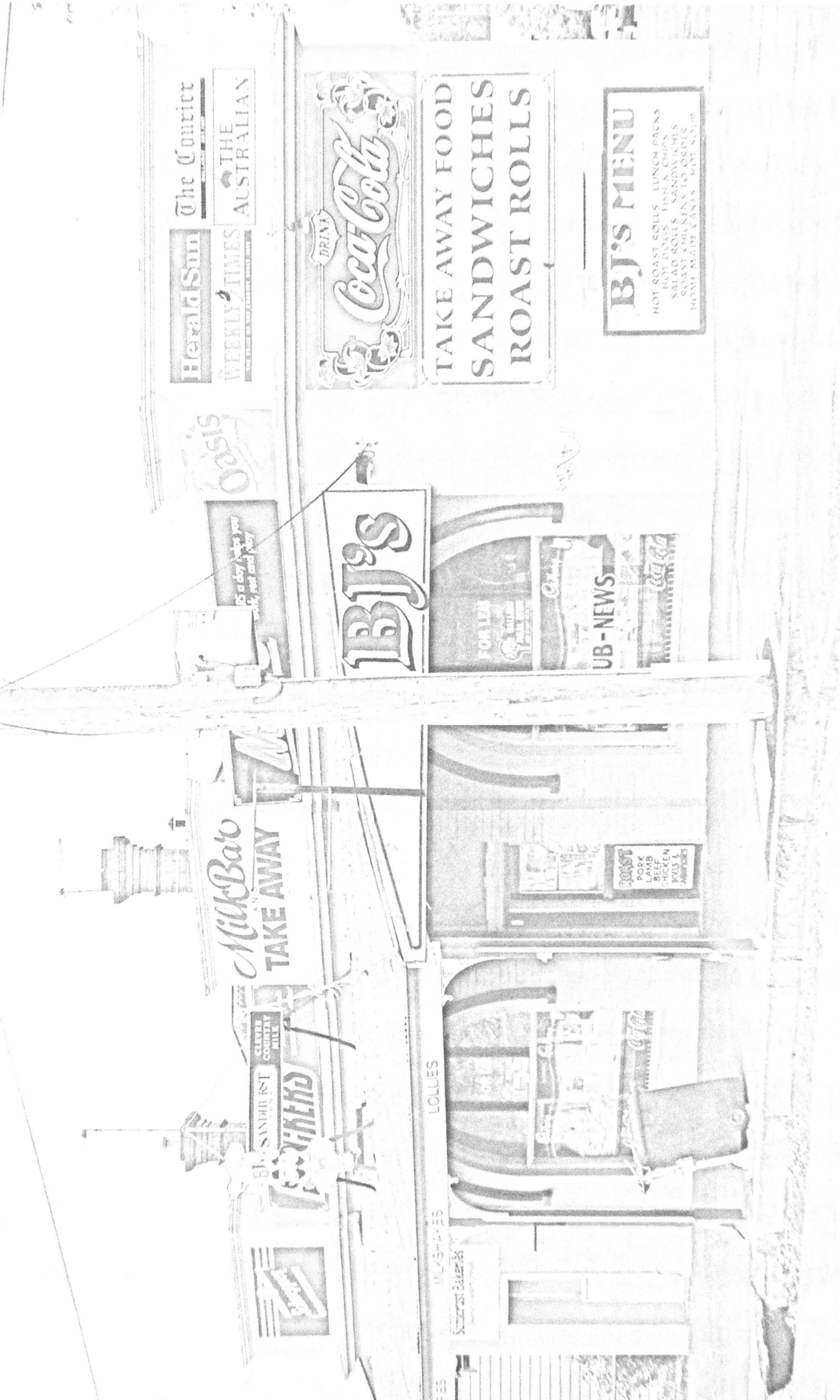

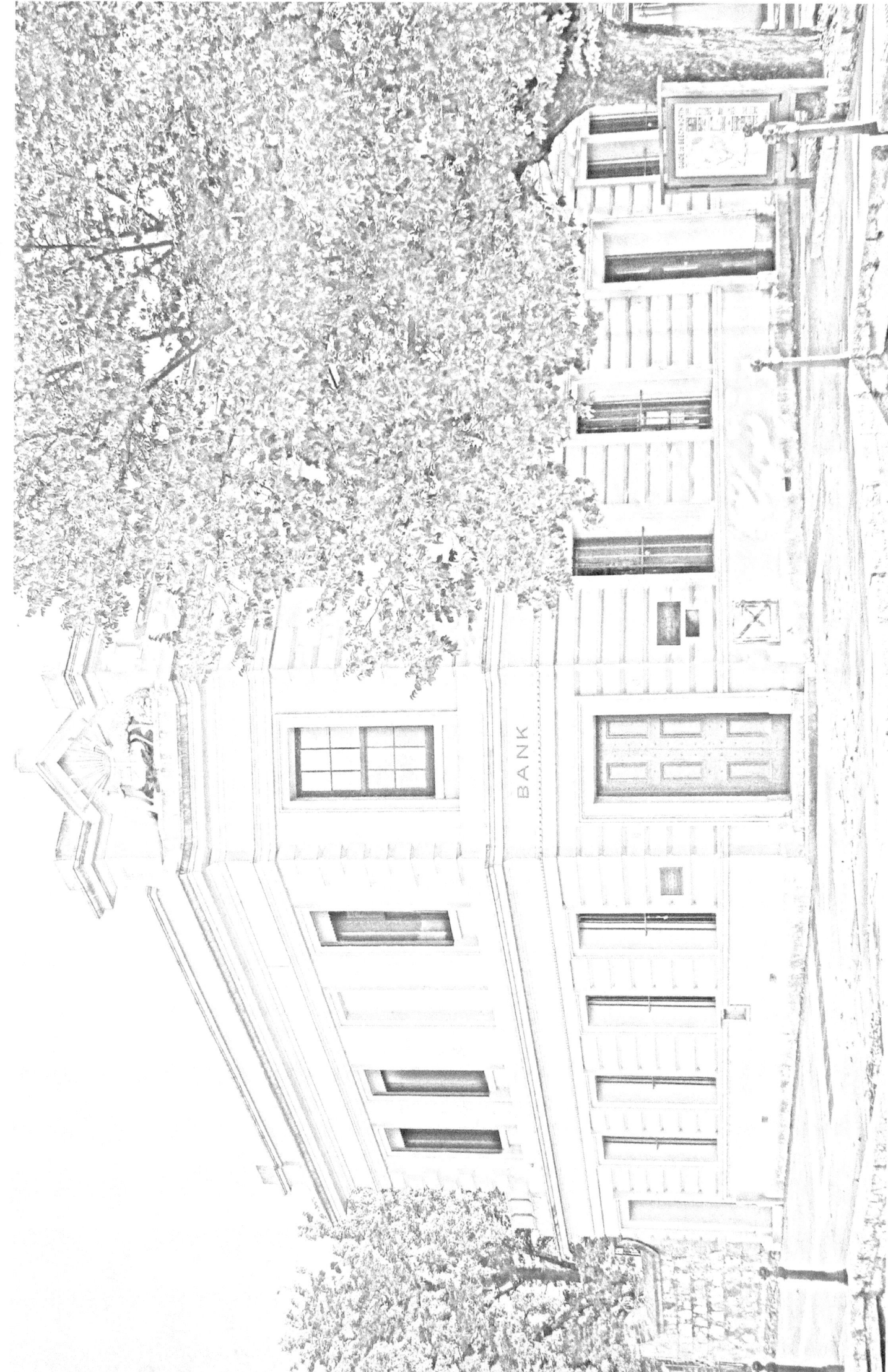

Bats

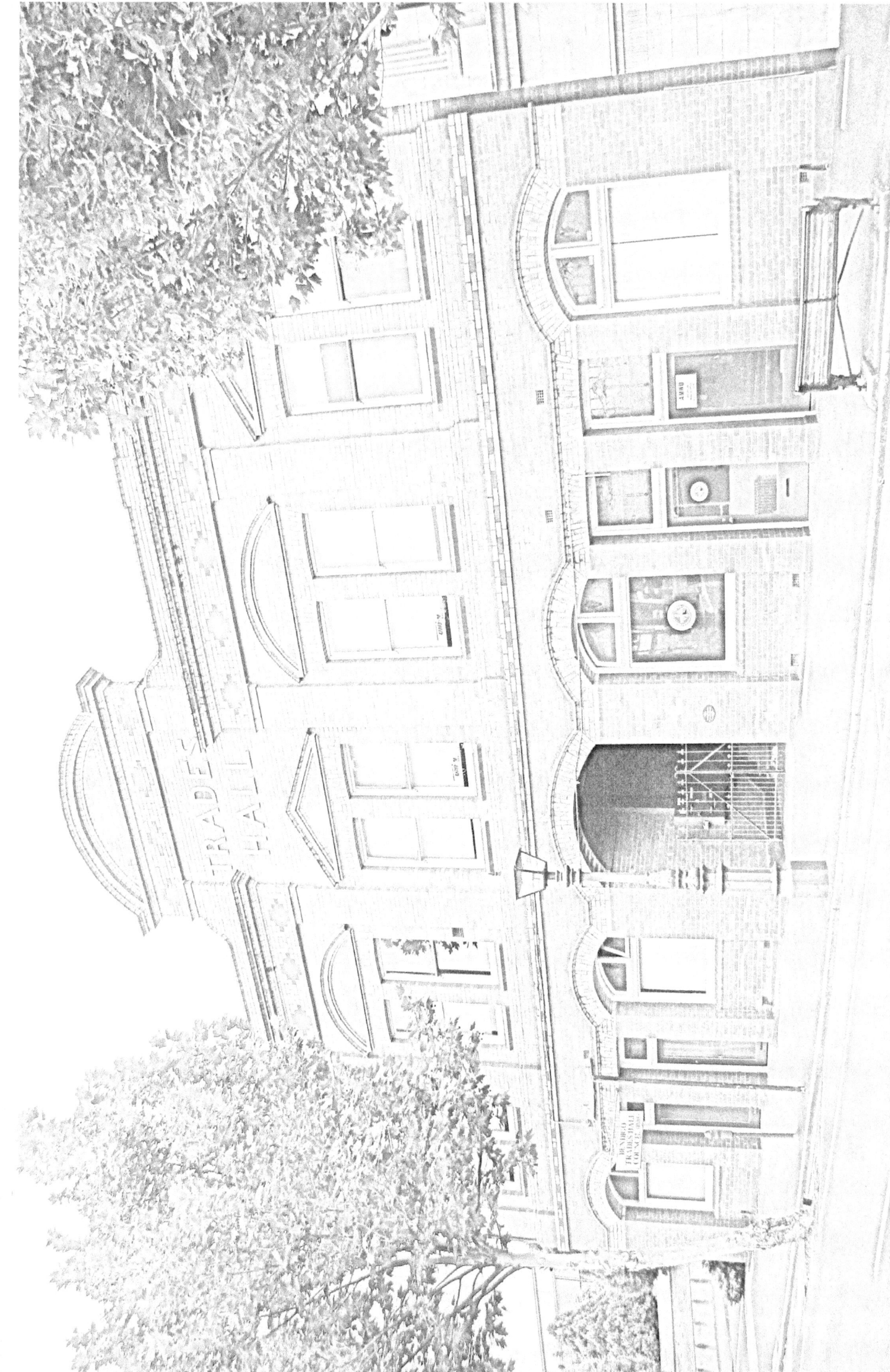

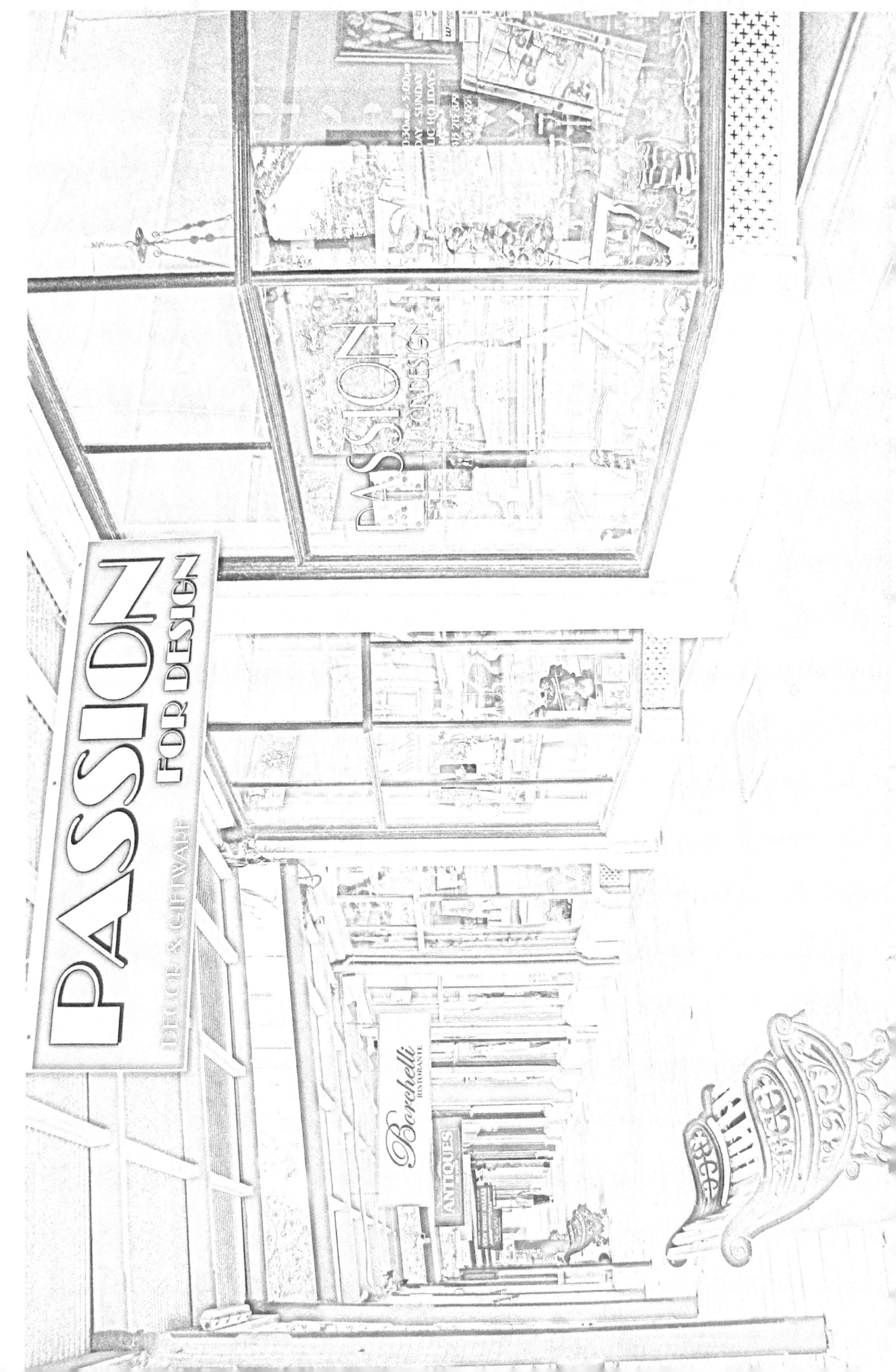

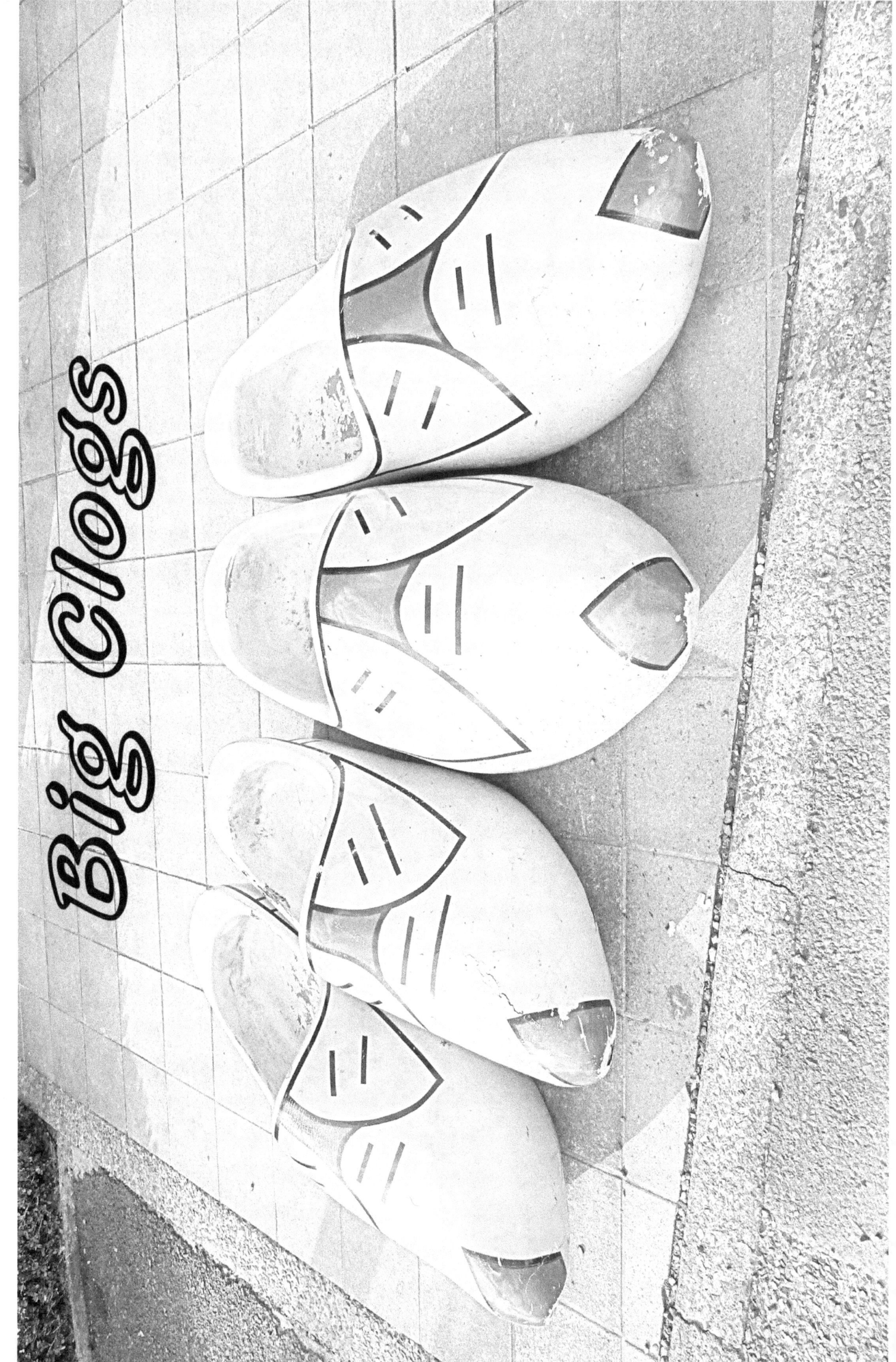

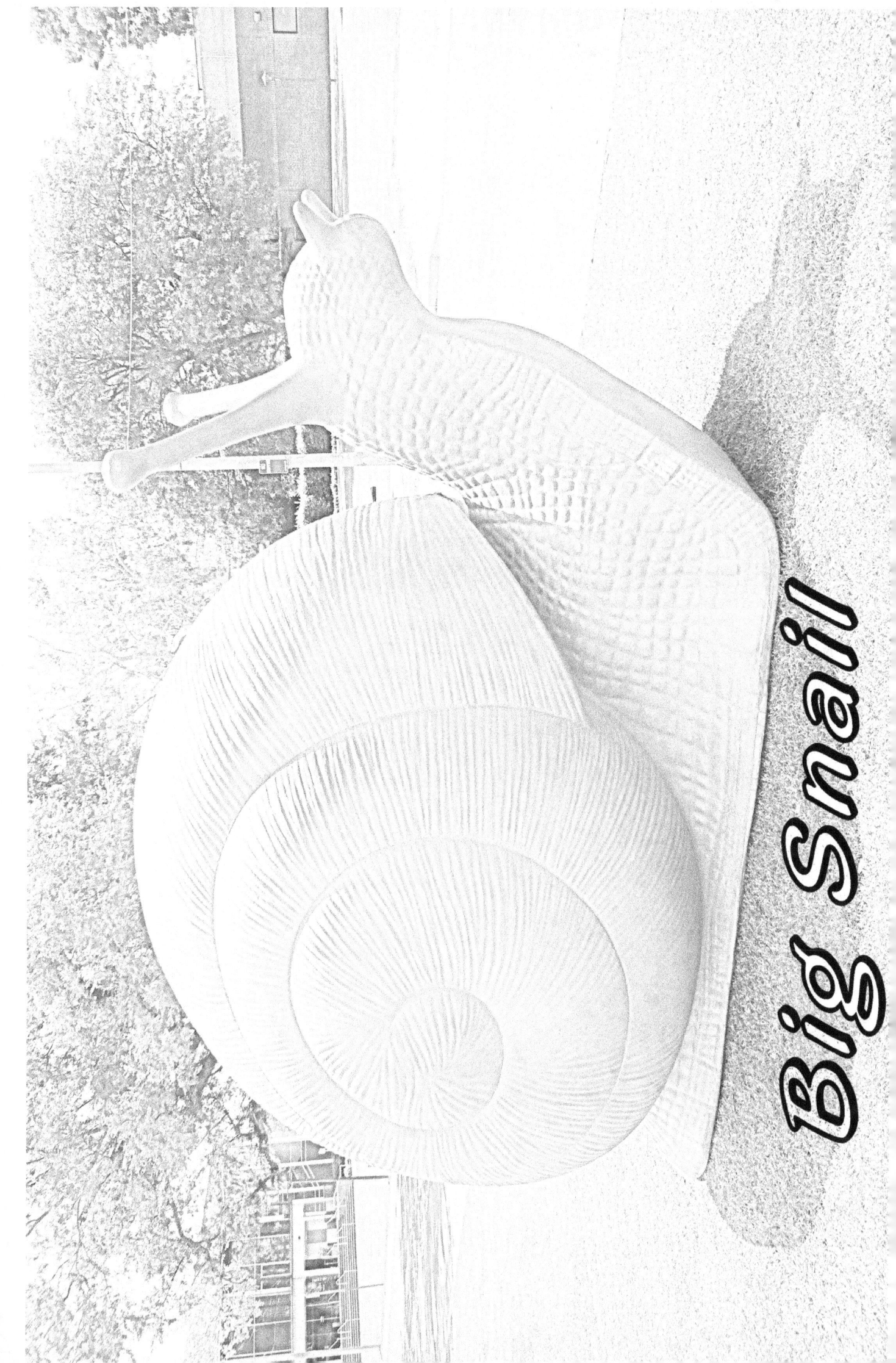

Big Snail

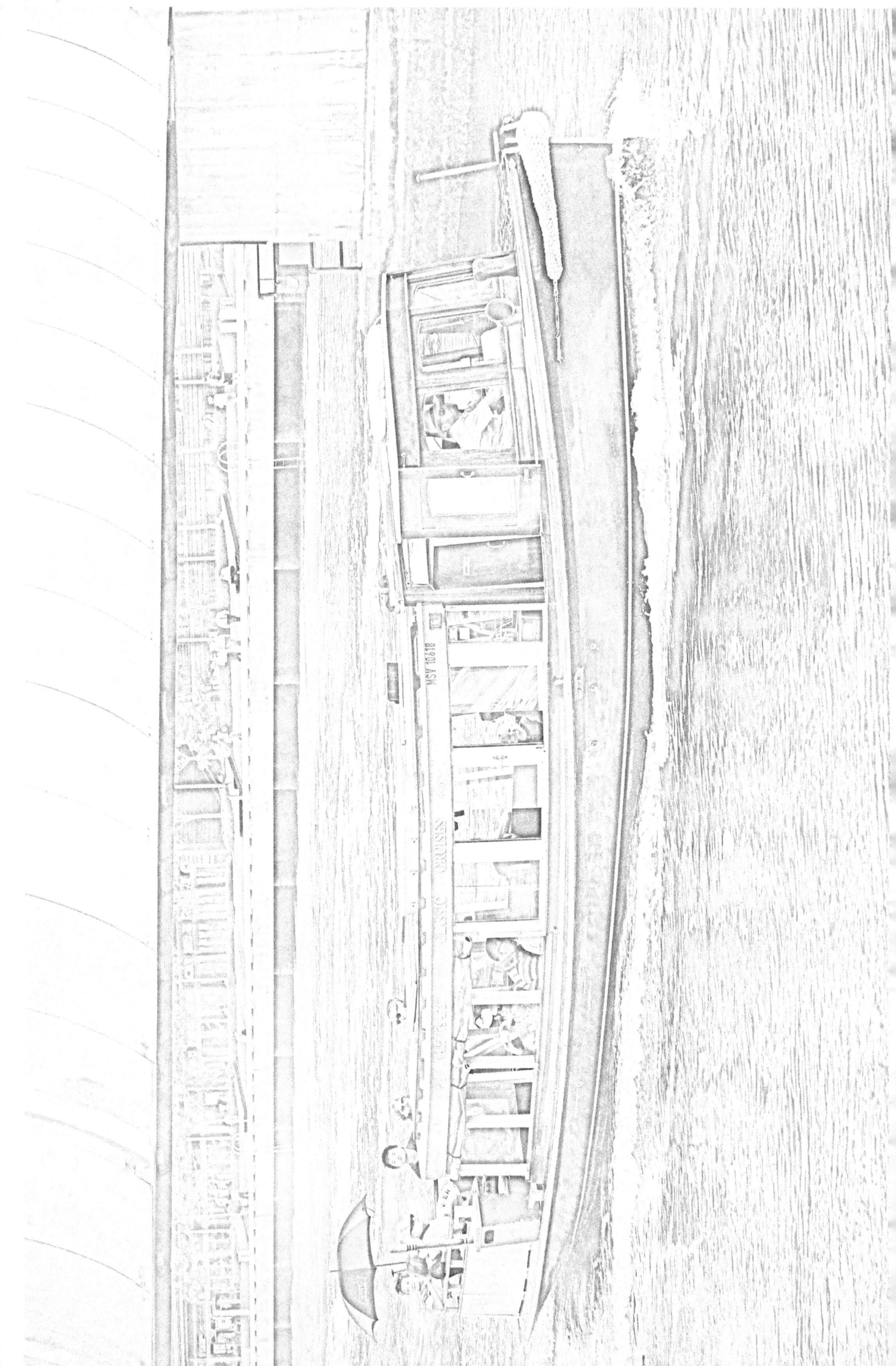

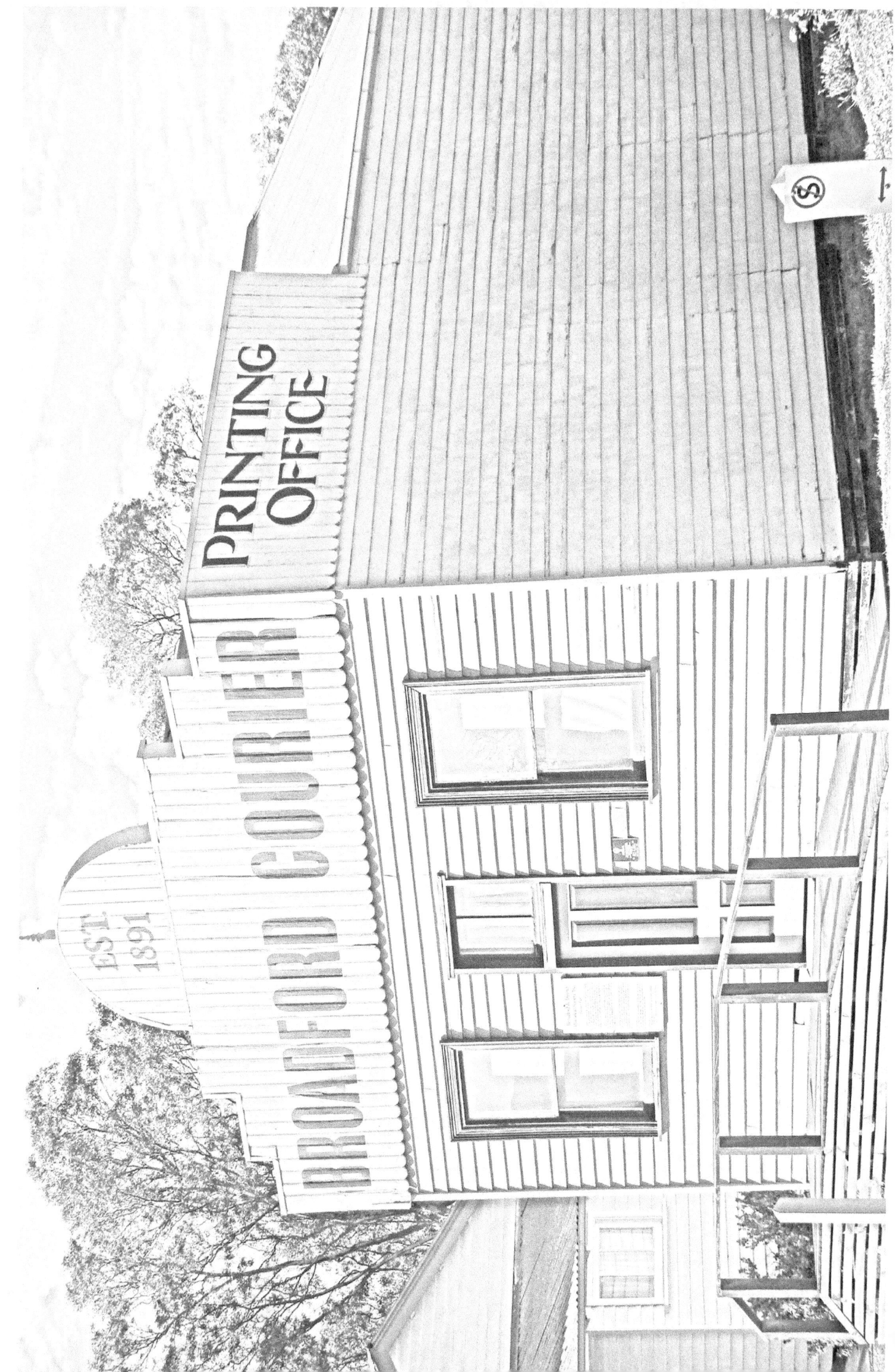

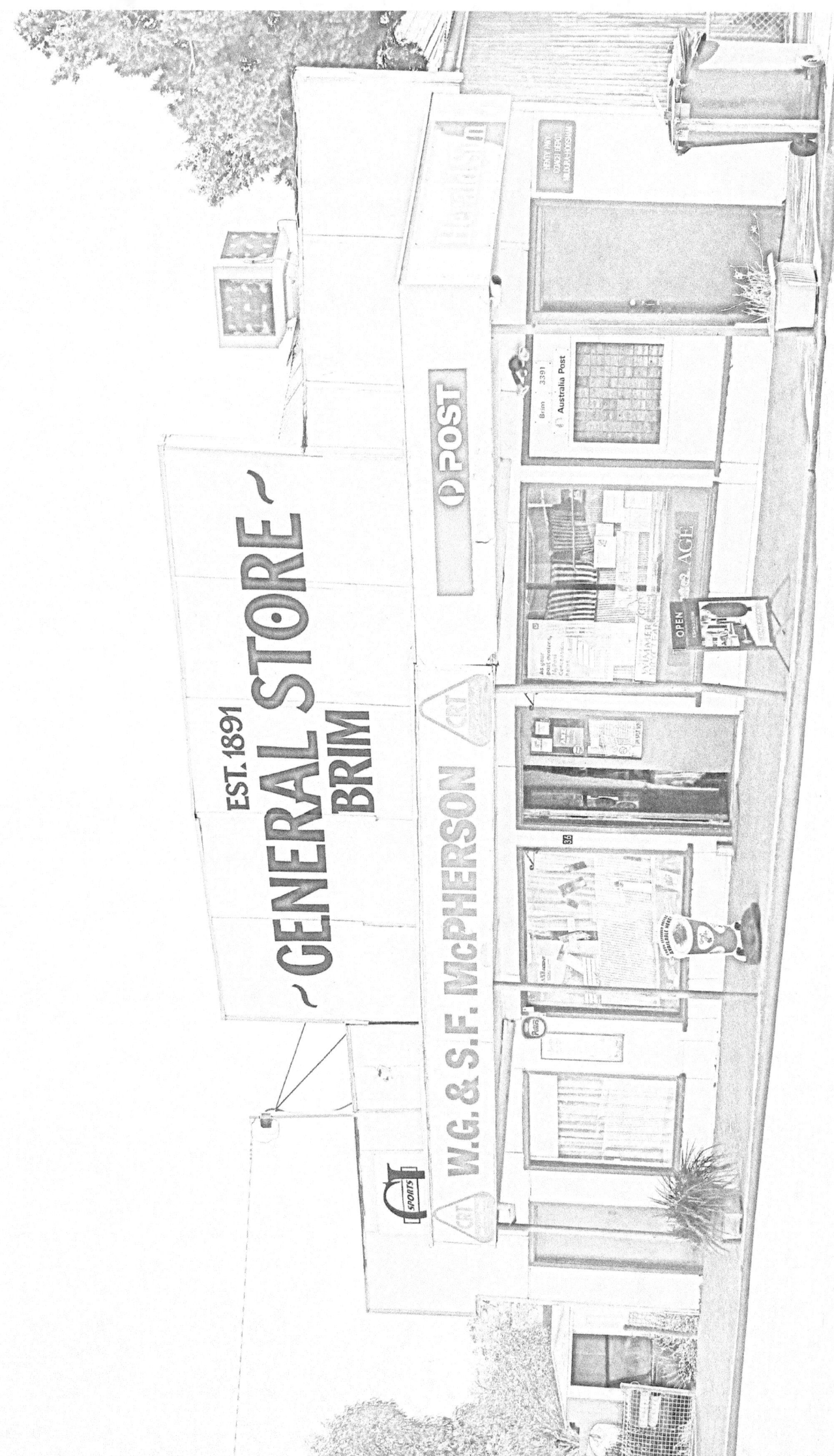

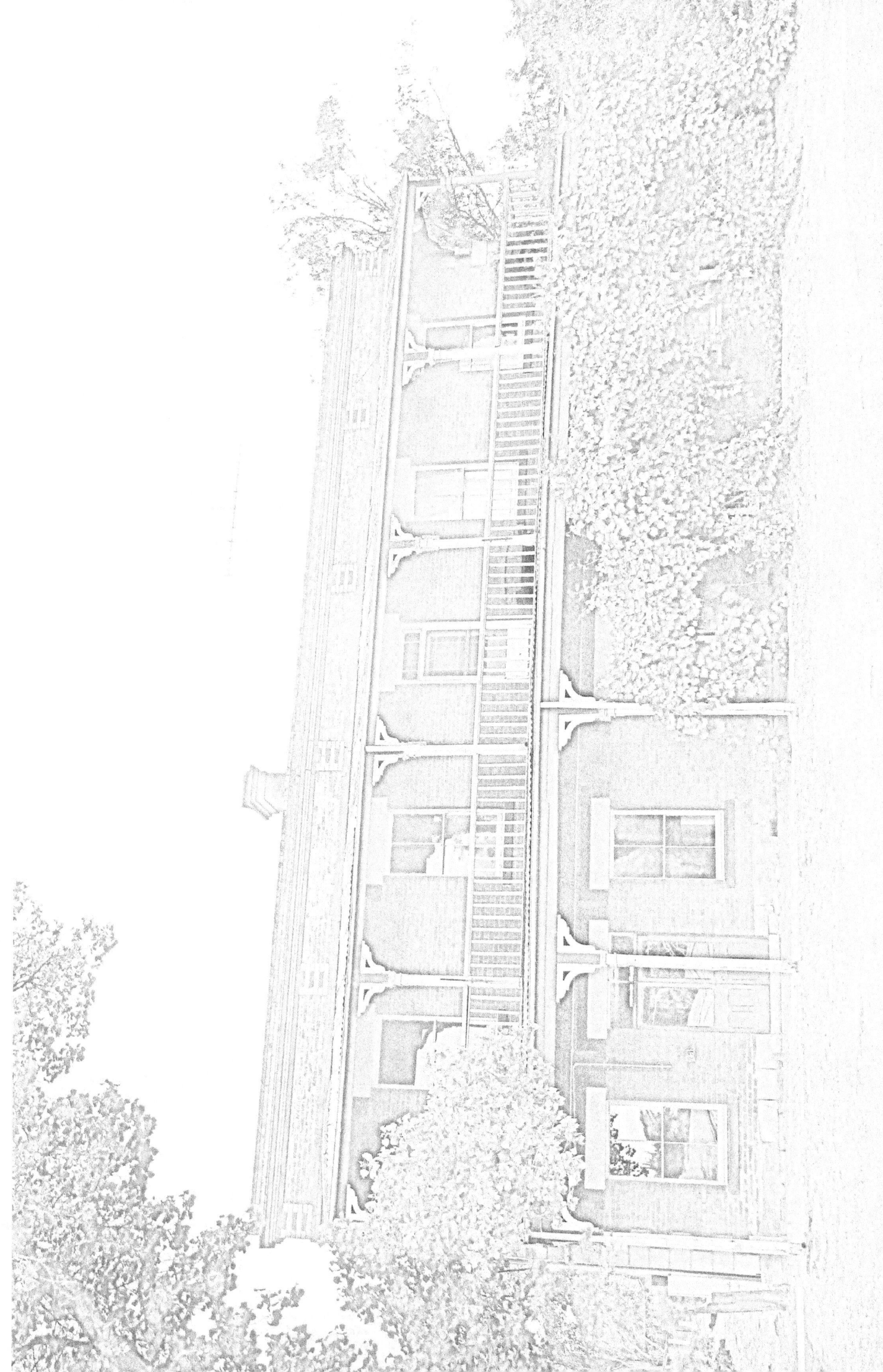

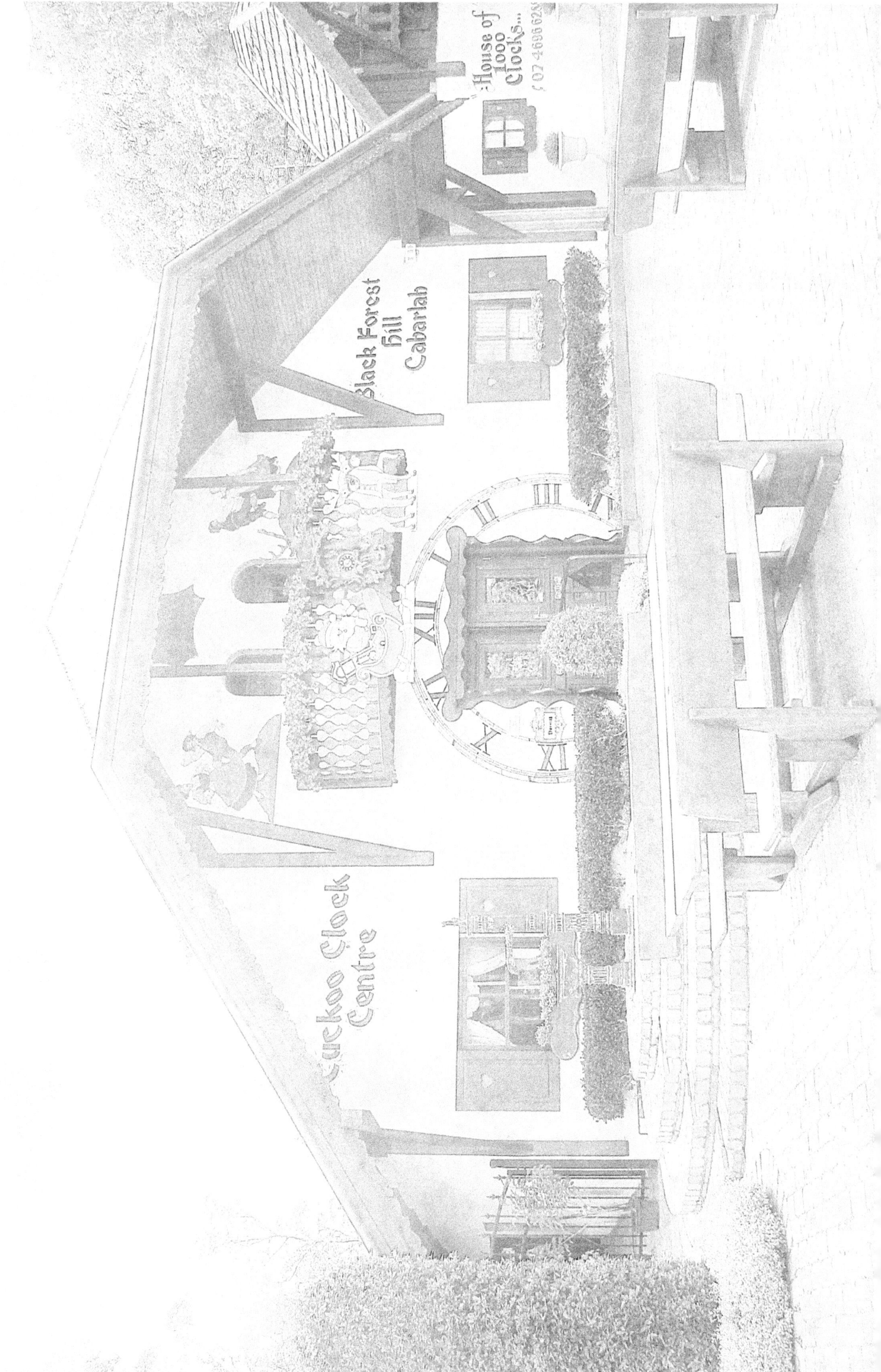

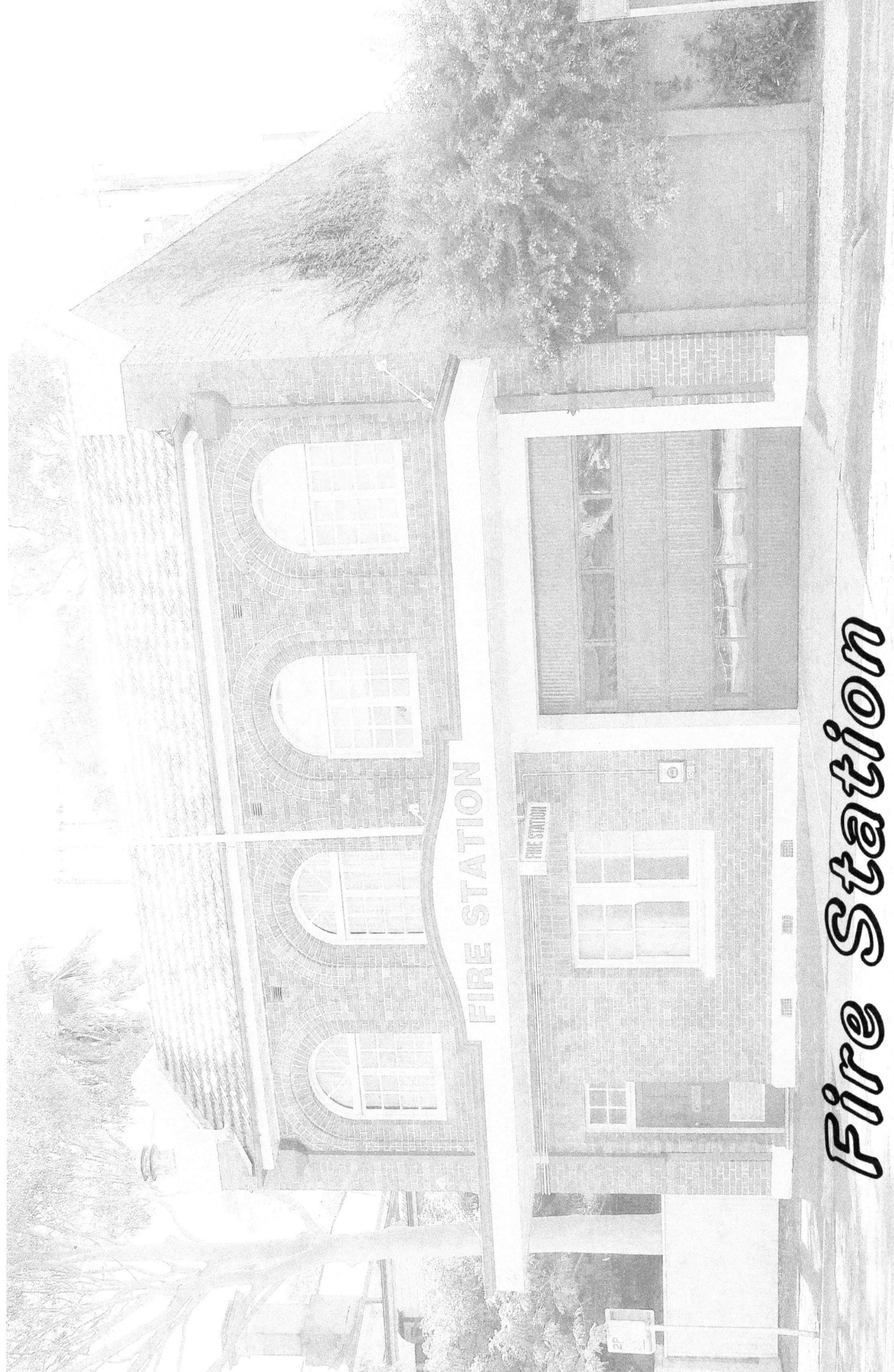

Fire Station

Fire Station

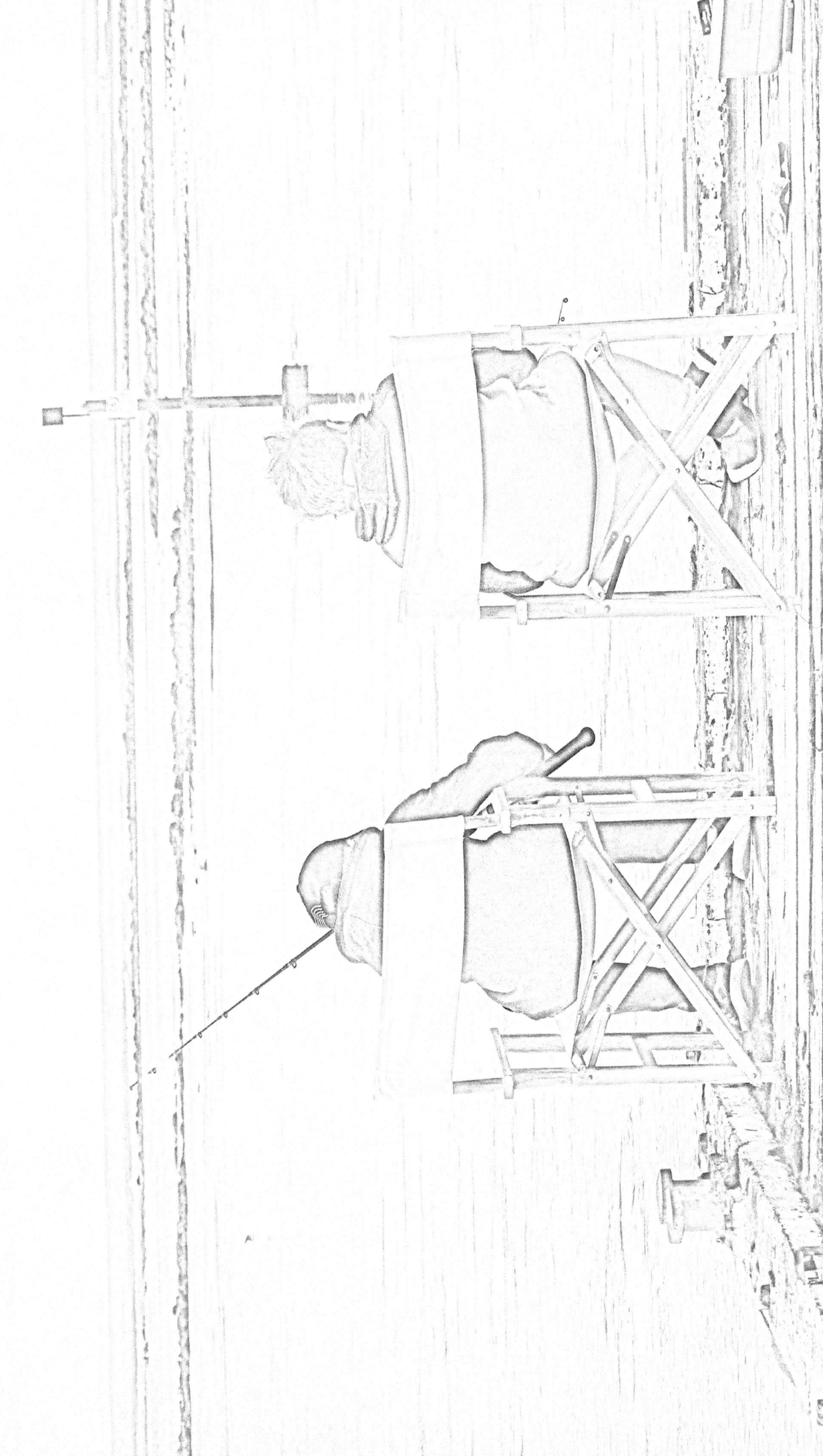

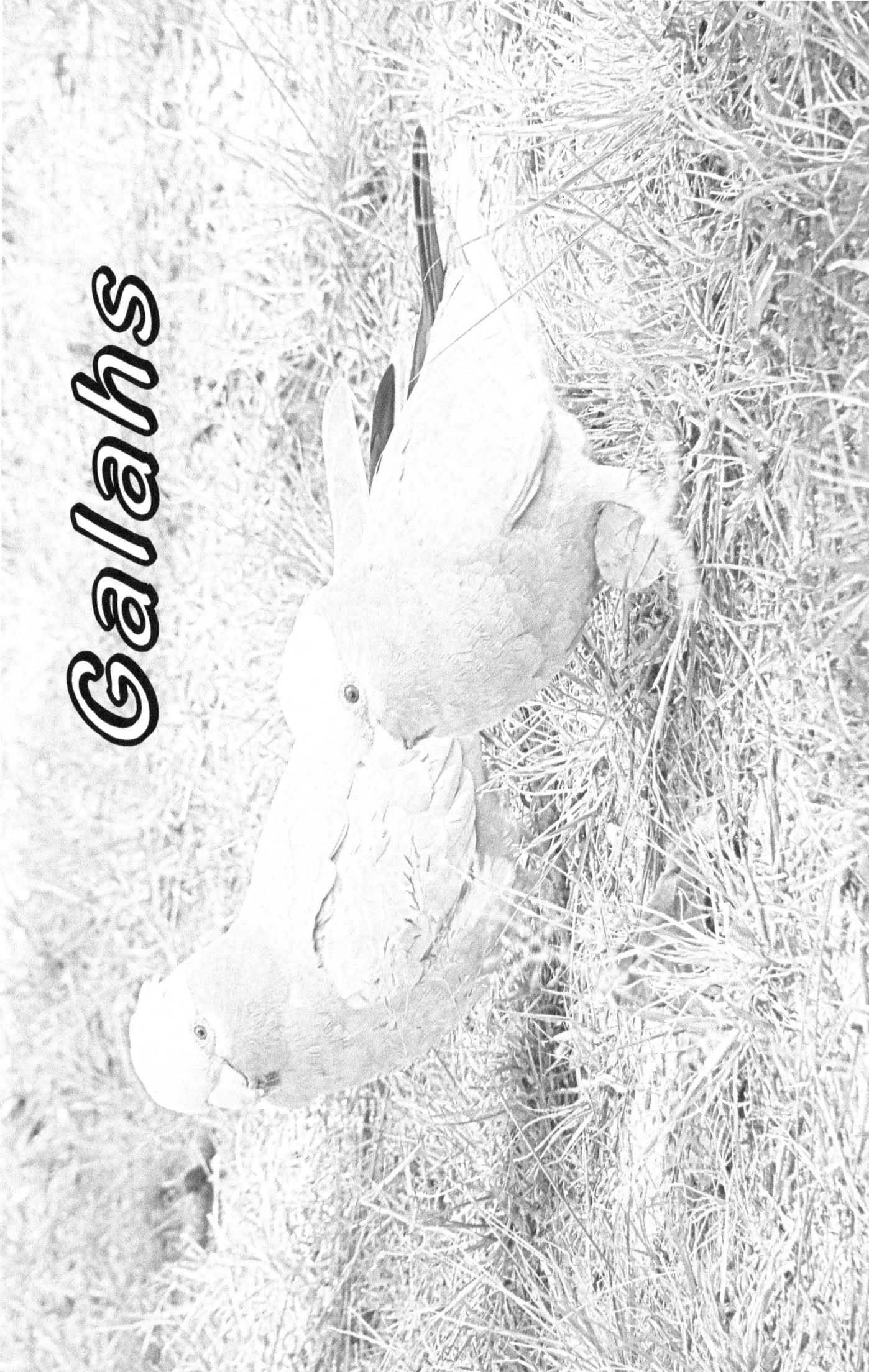

Galahs

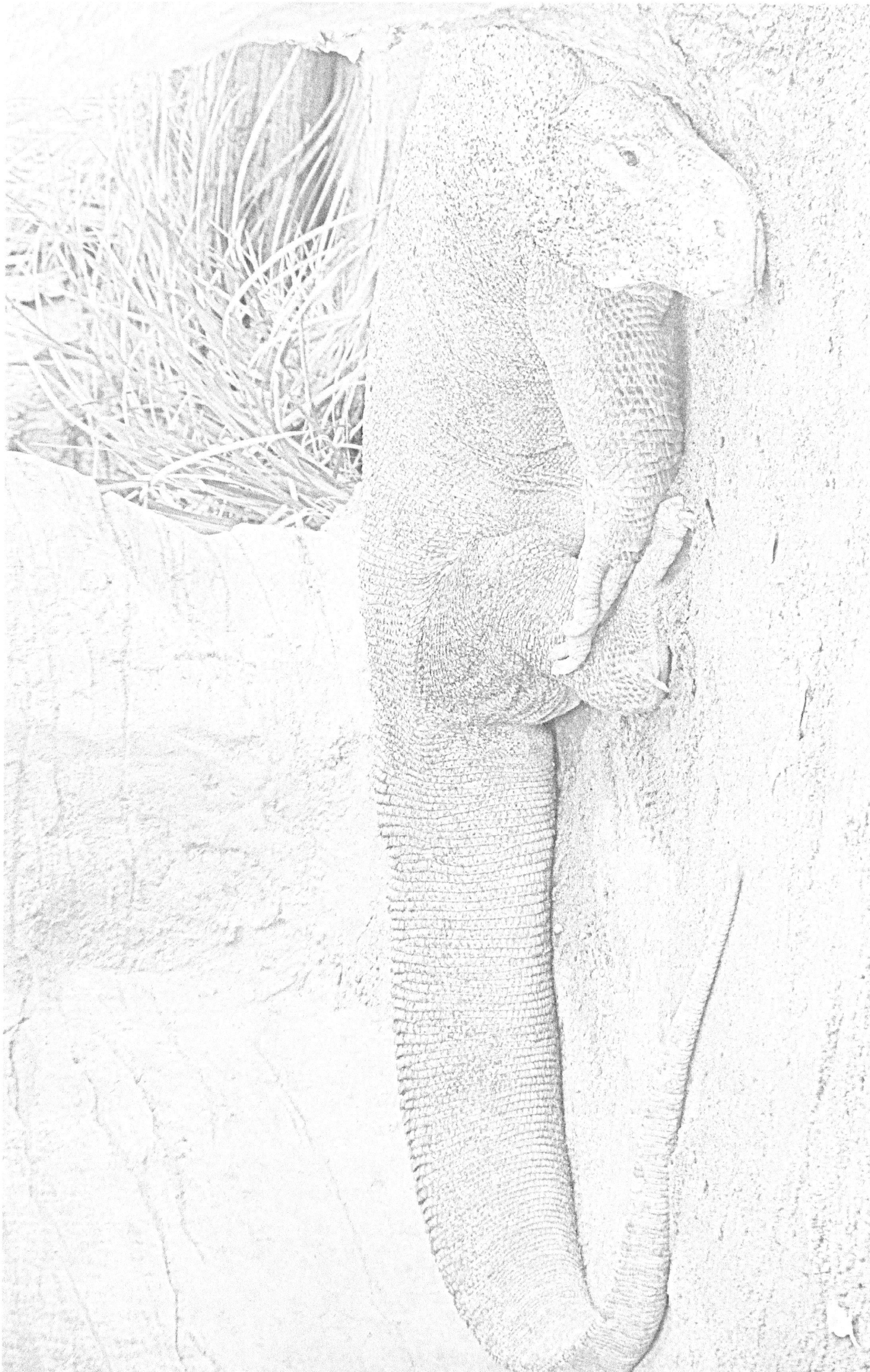

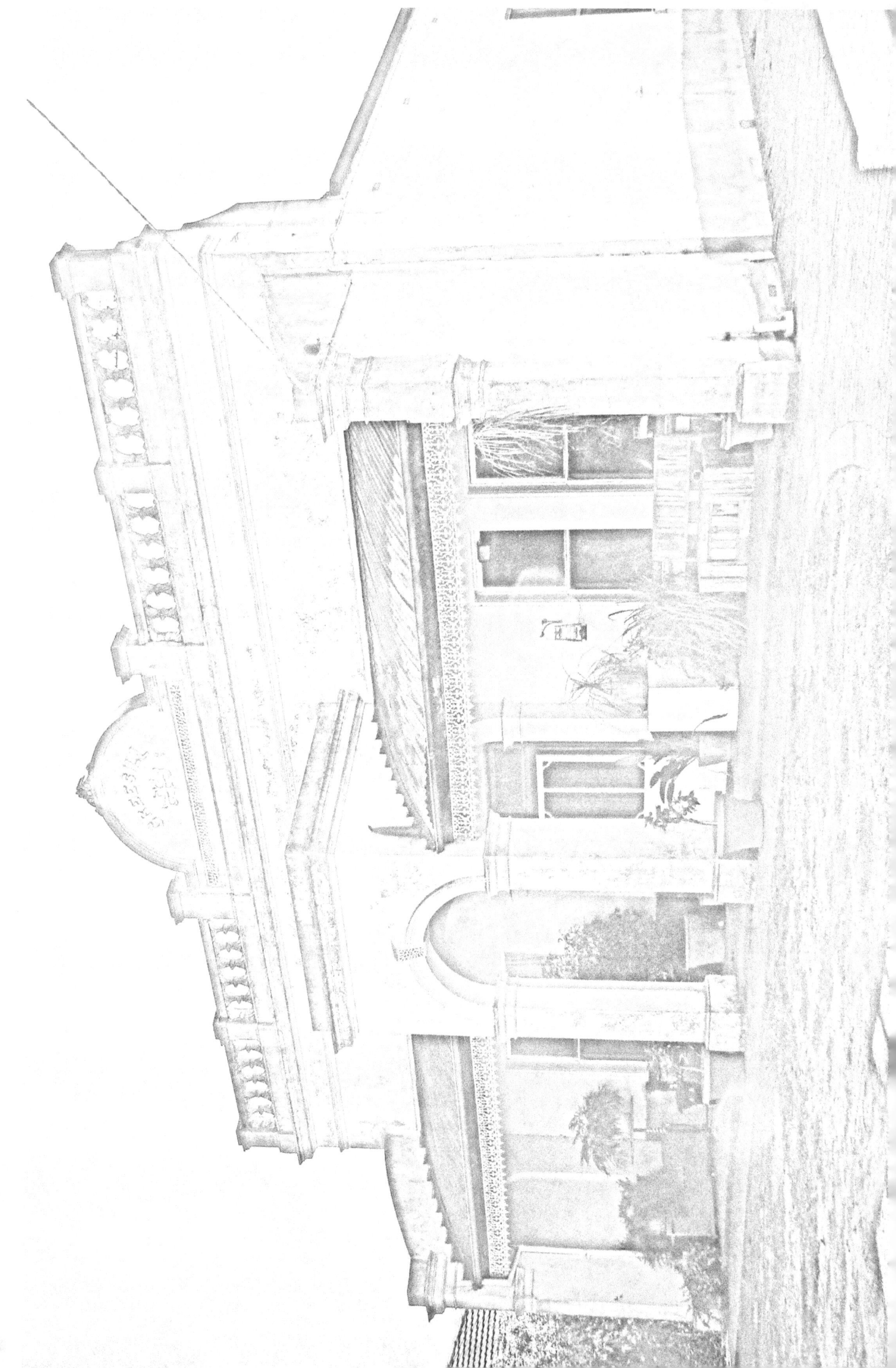

Hotel

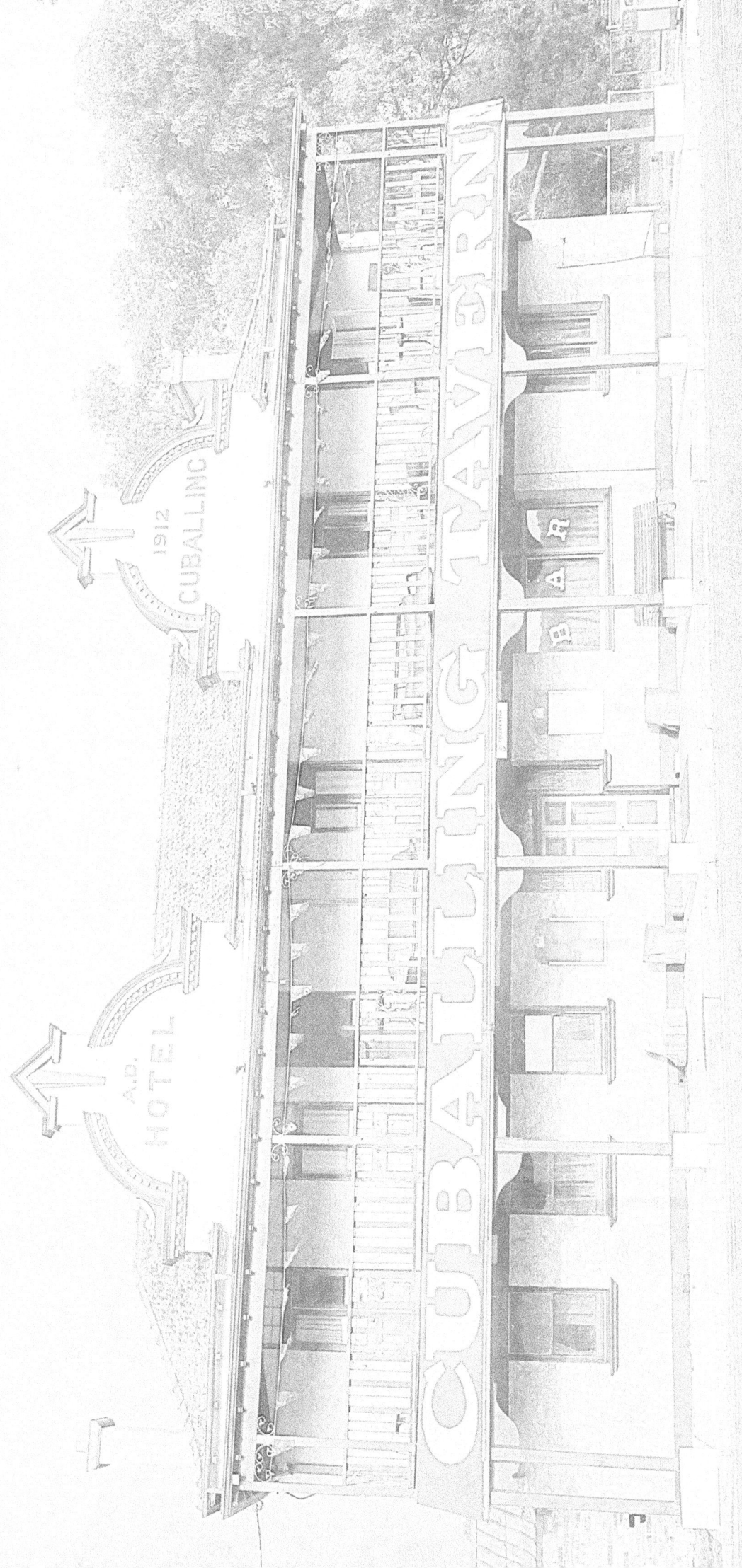

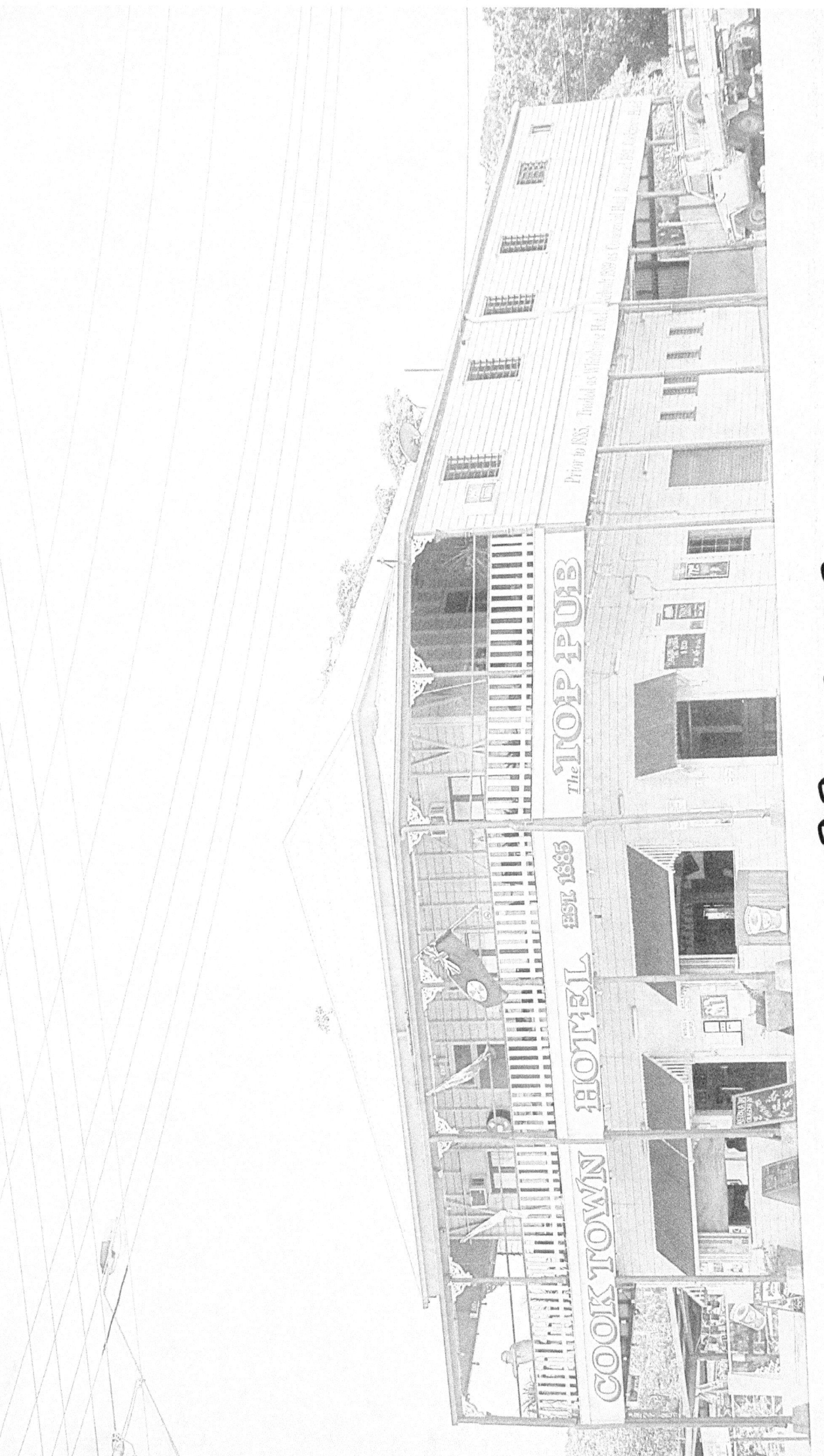

Hotel

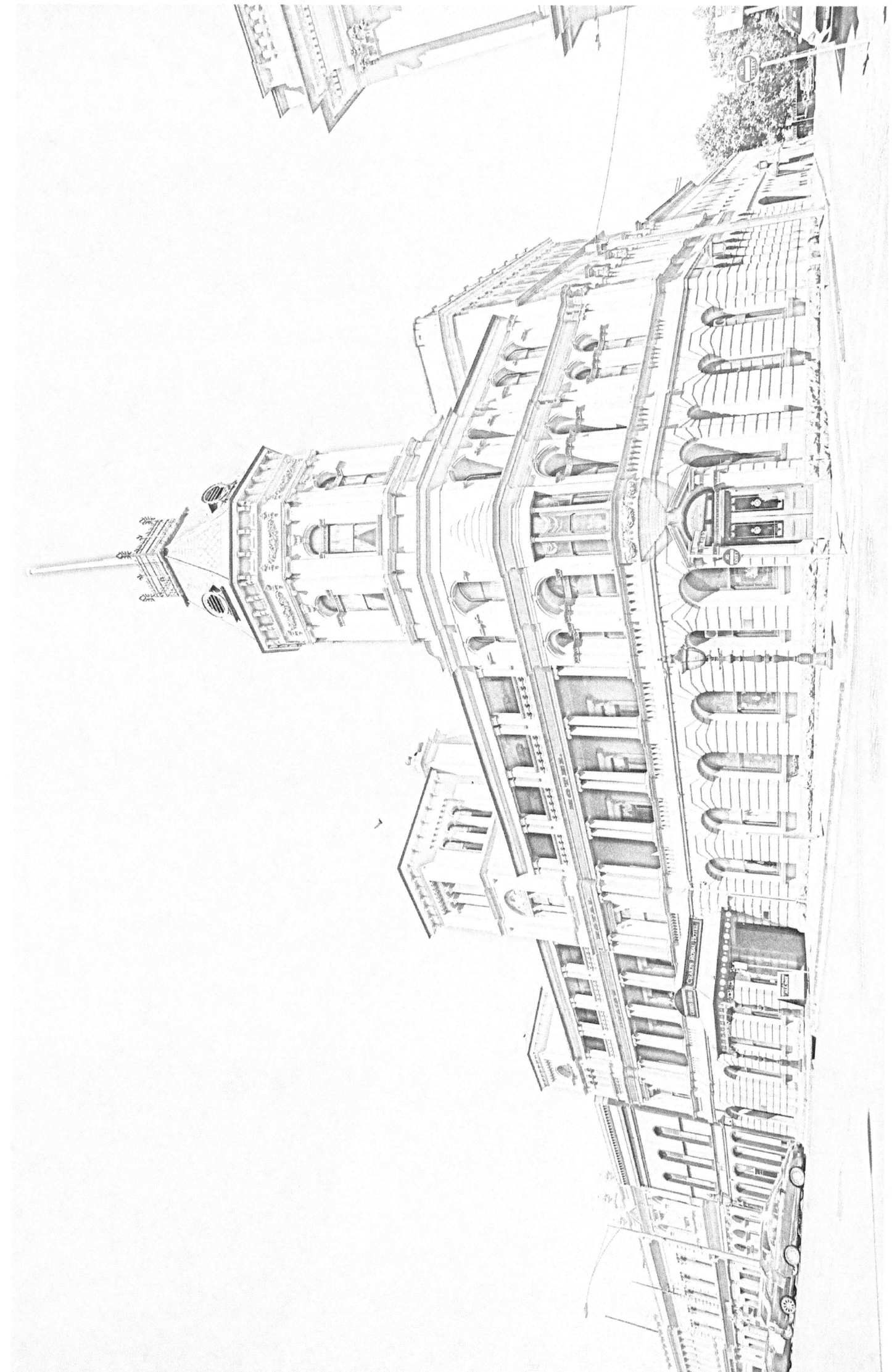

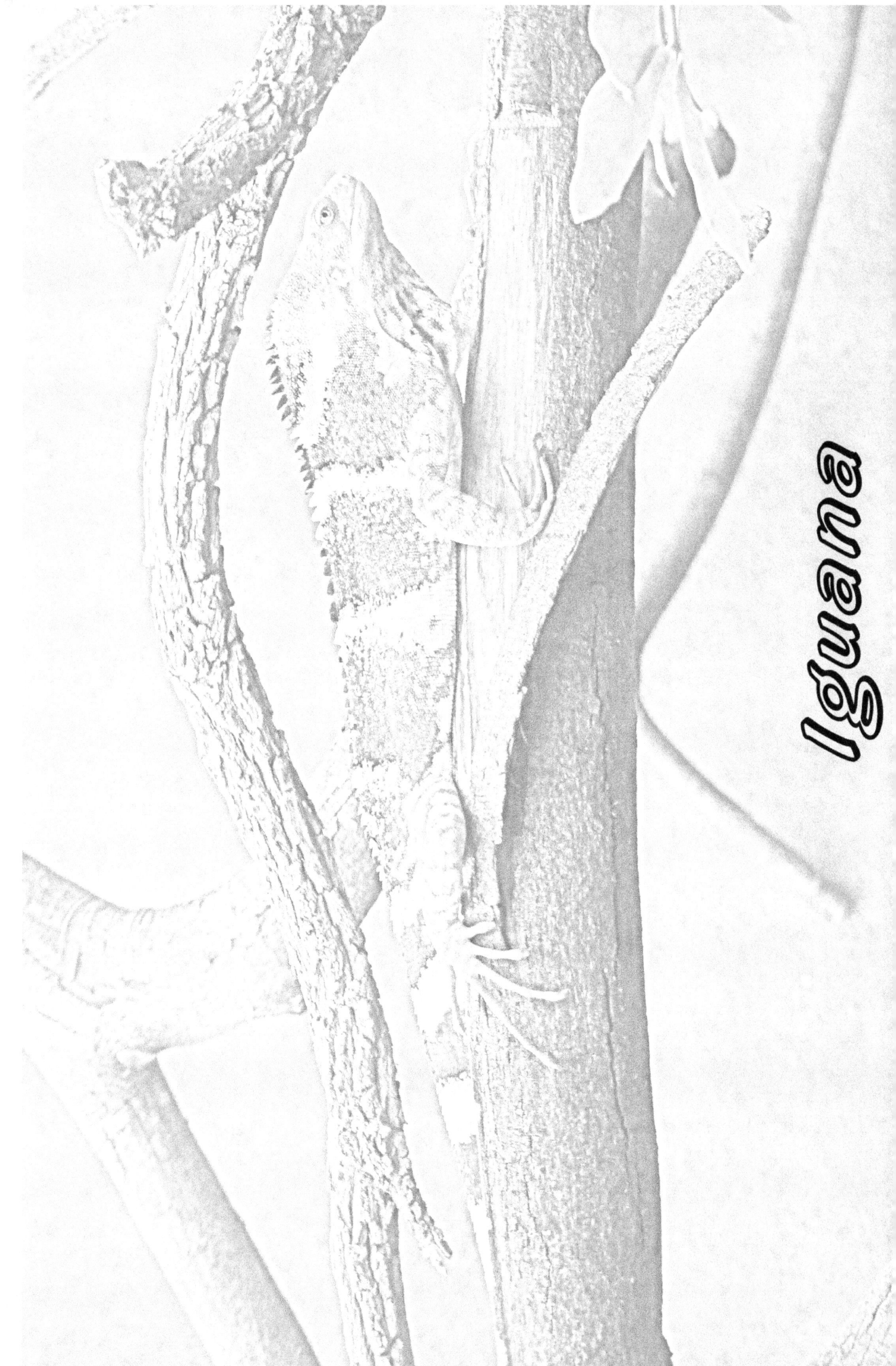

Iguana

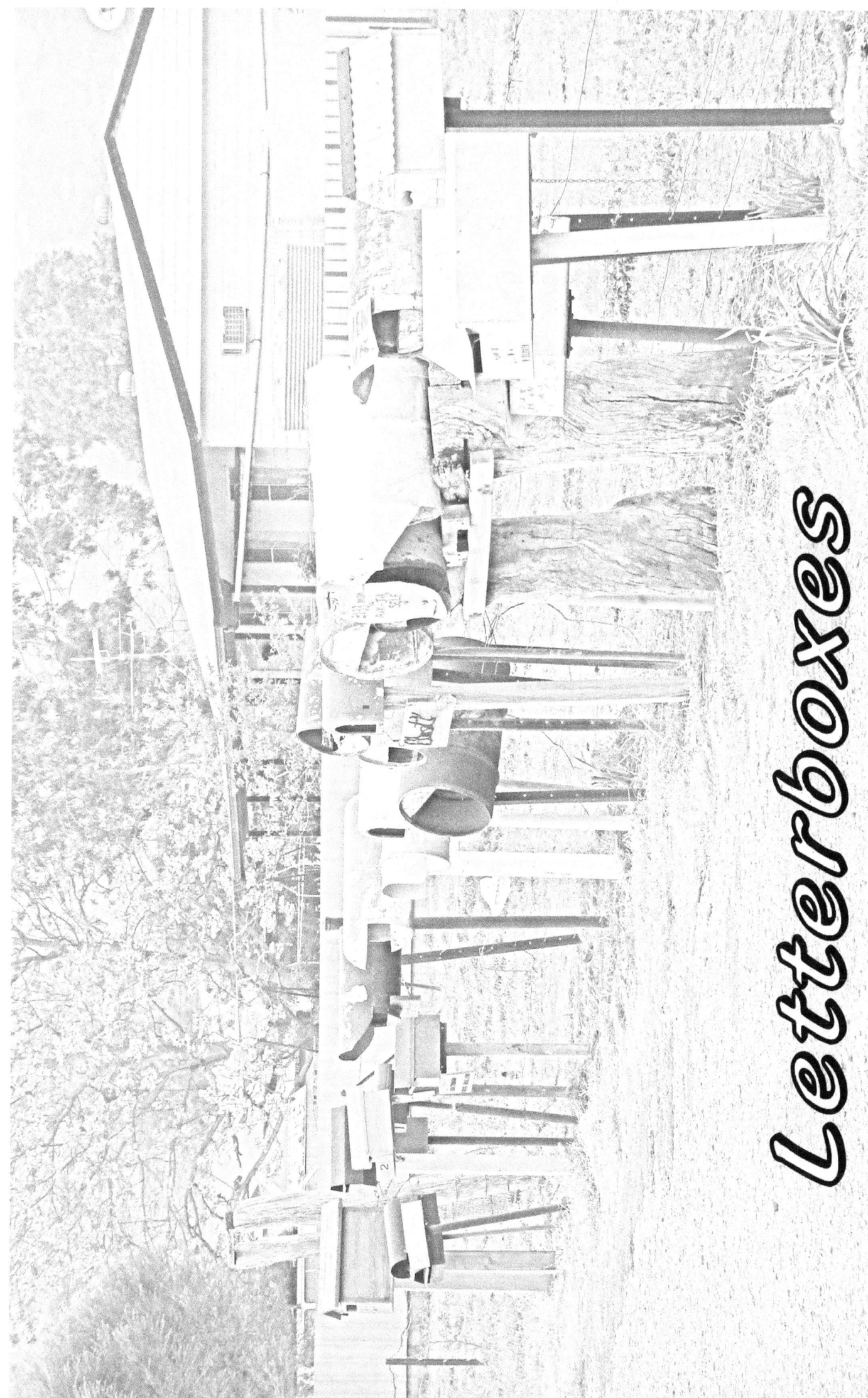

Letterboxes

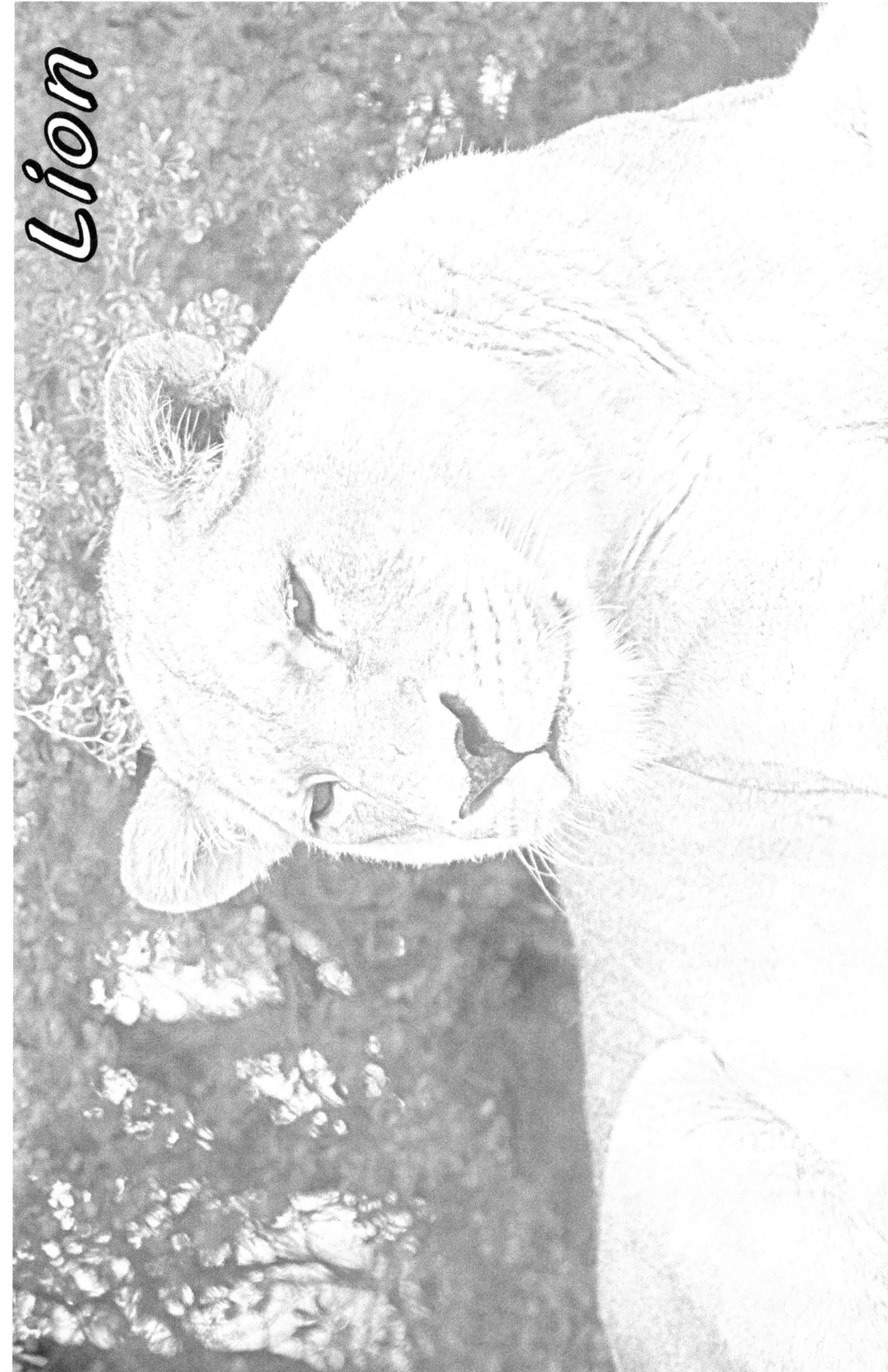

Lion

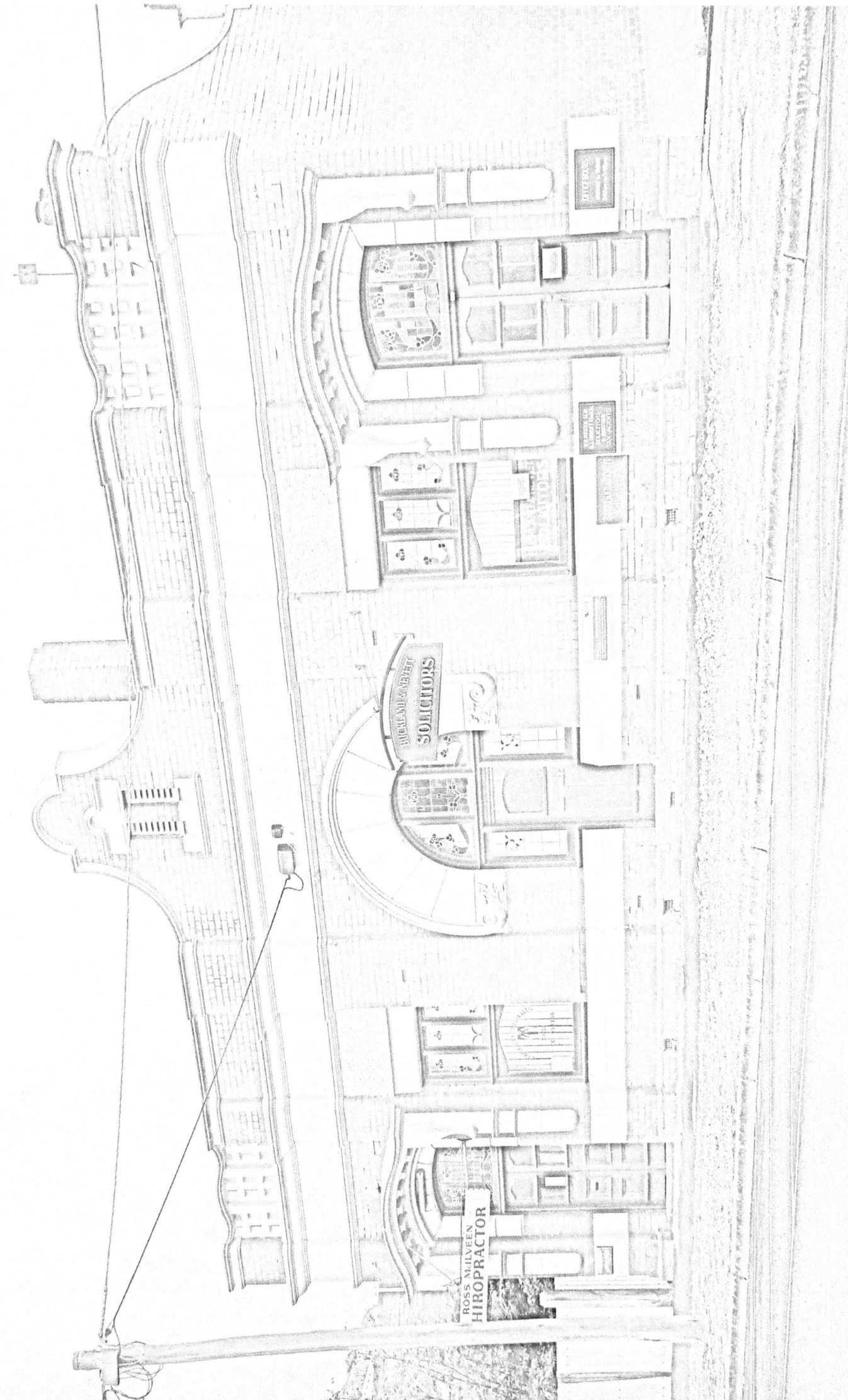

Pygmy Hippopotamus

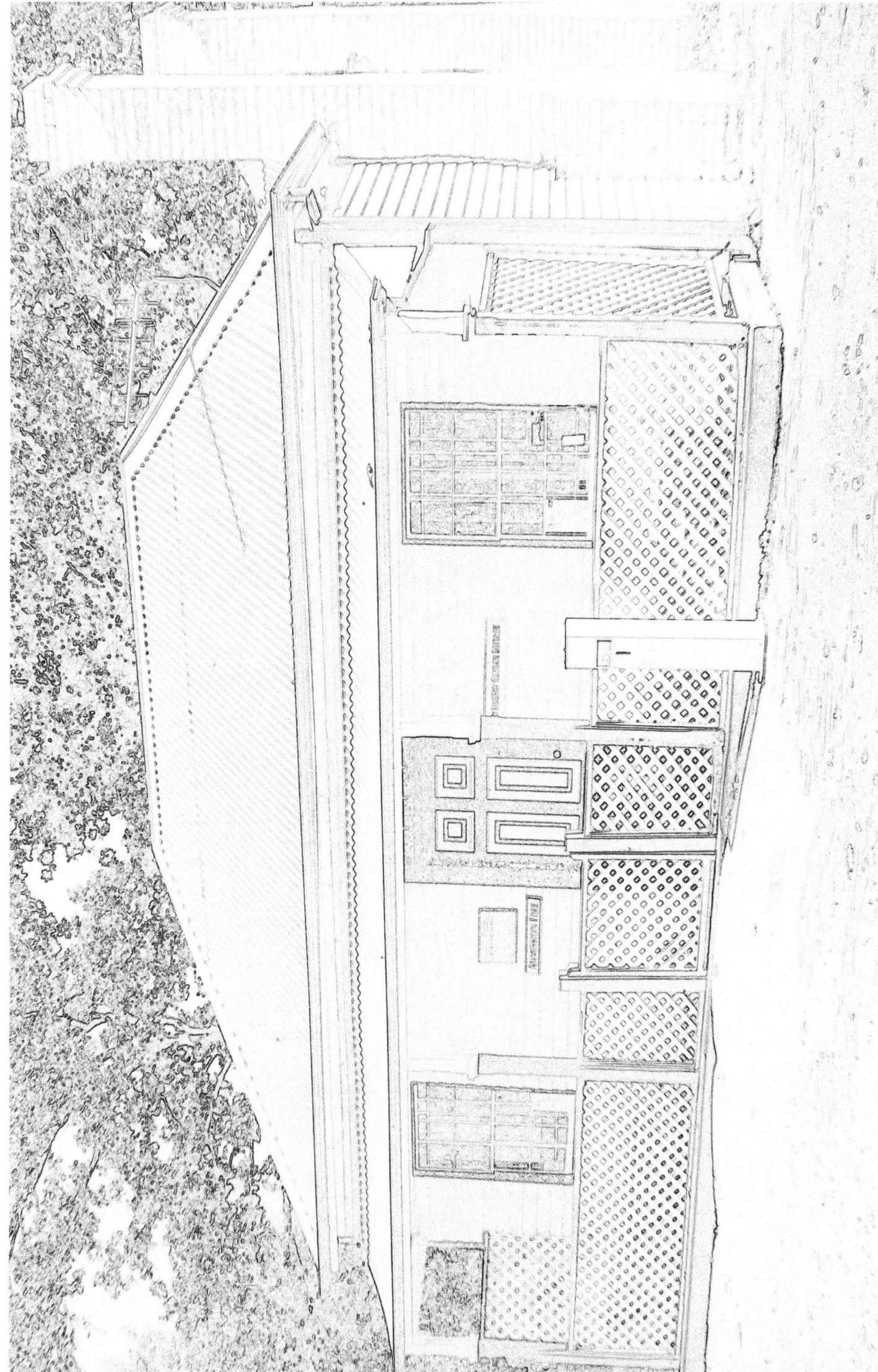

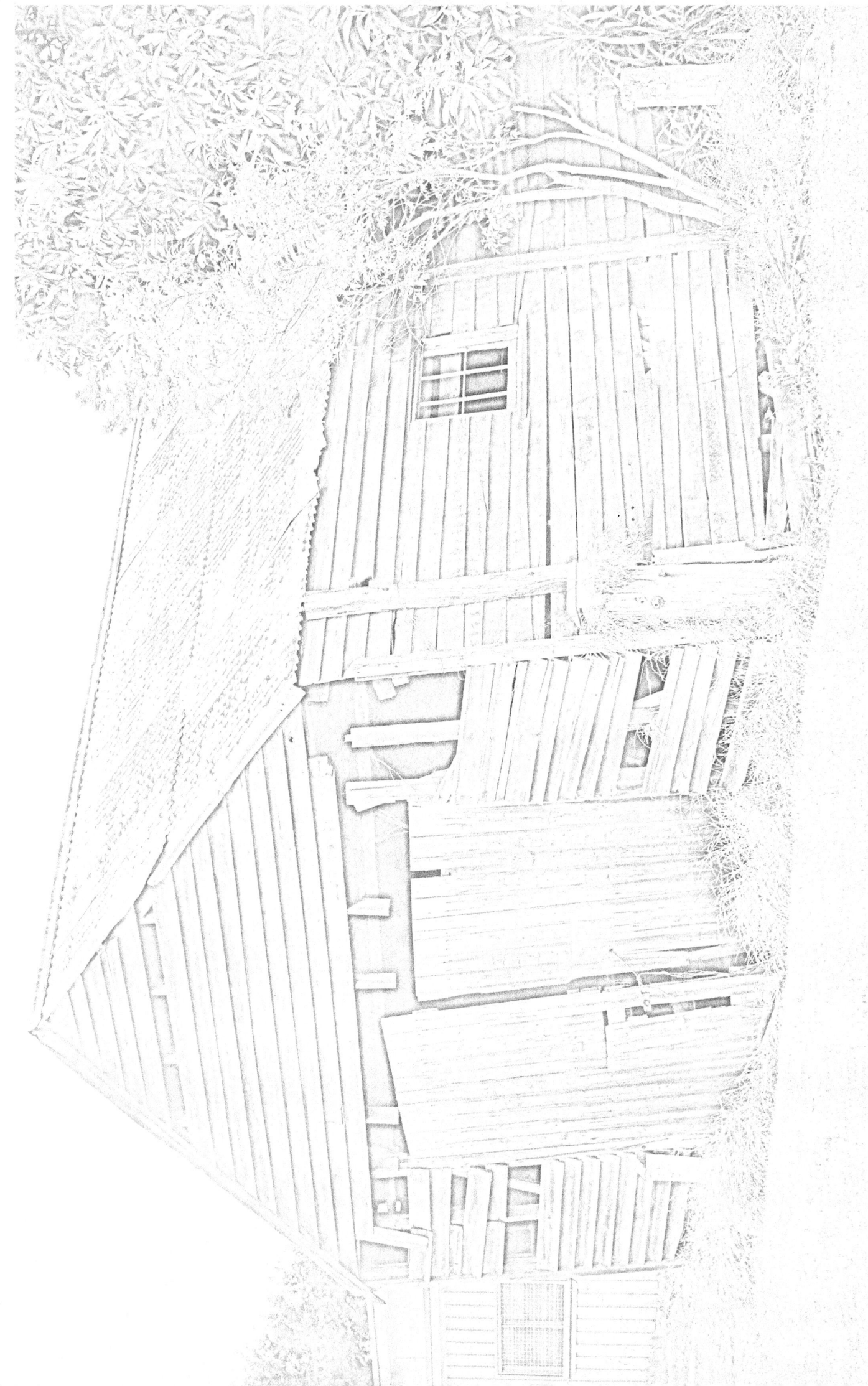

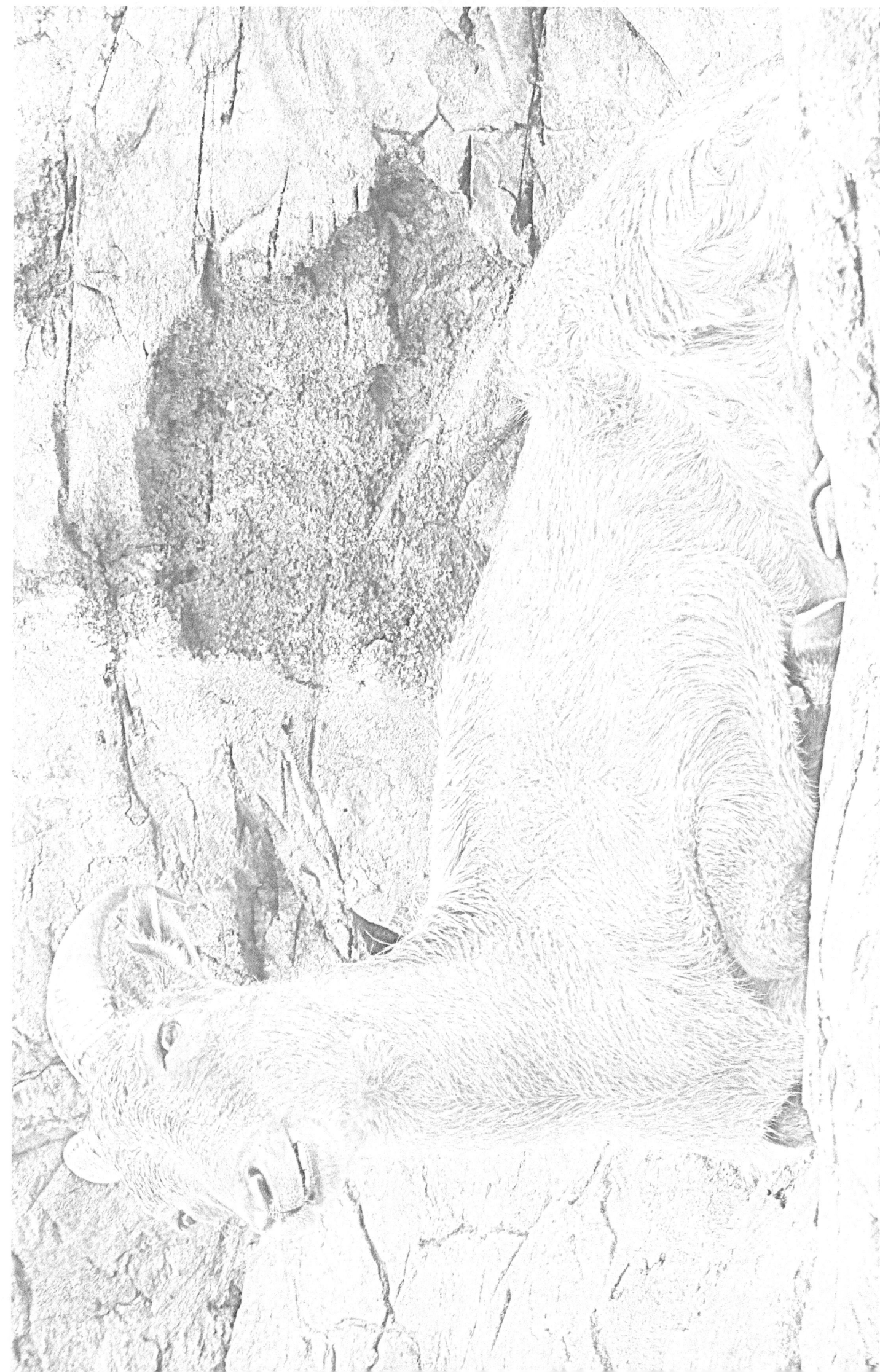

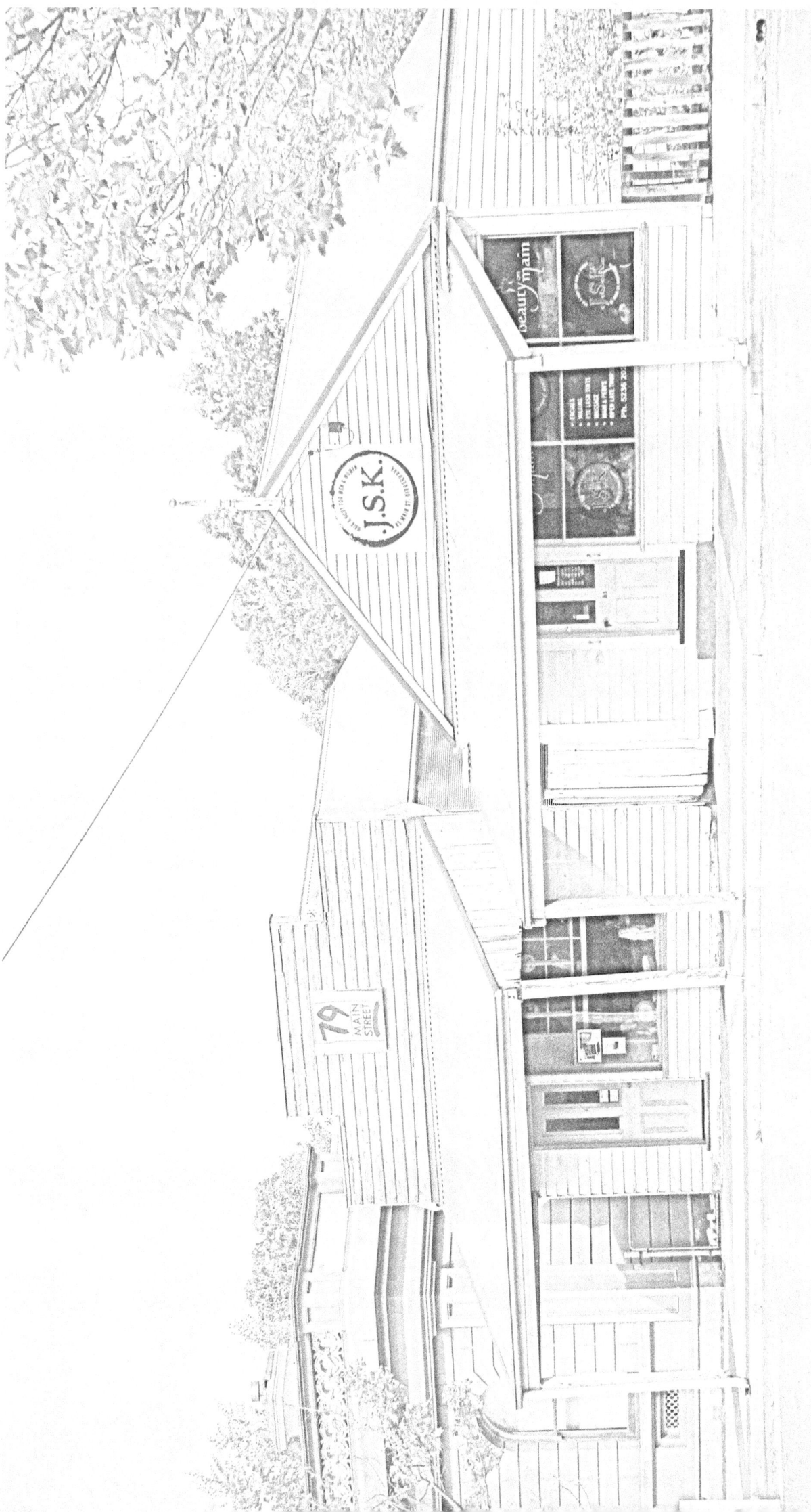

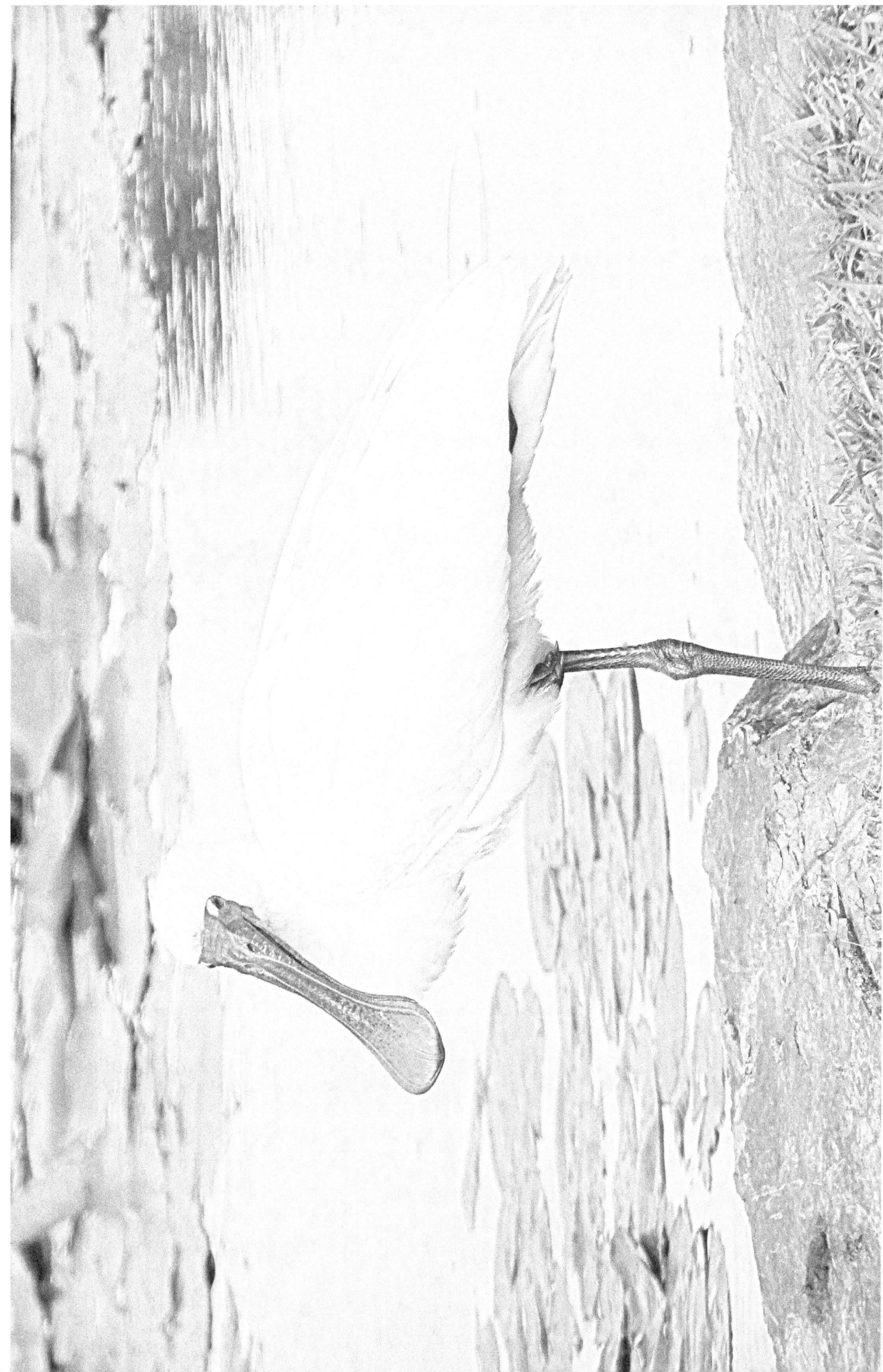

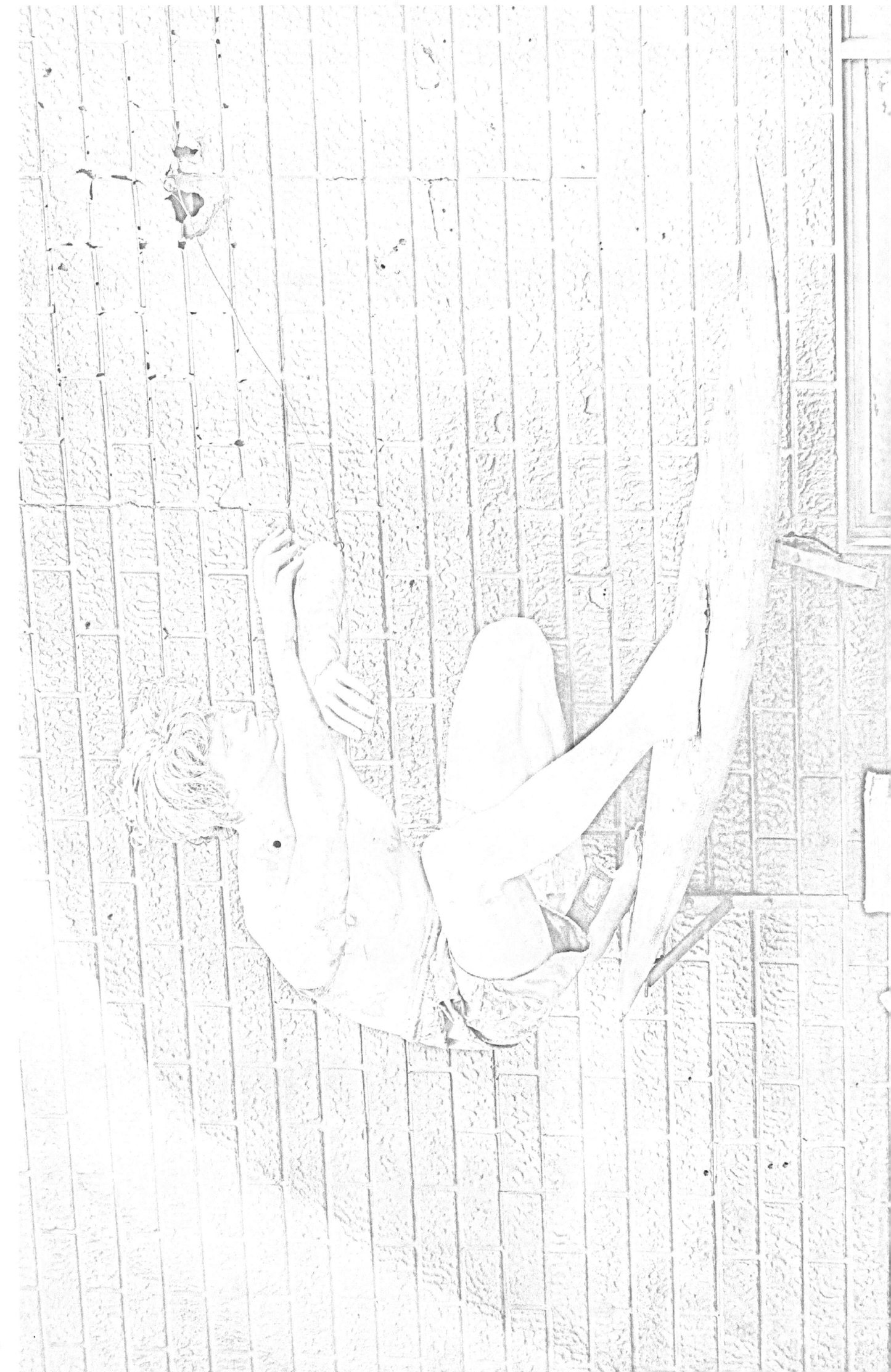

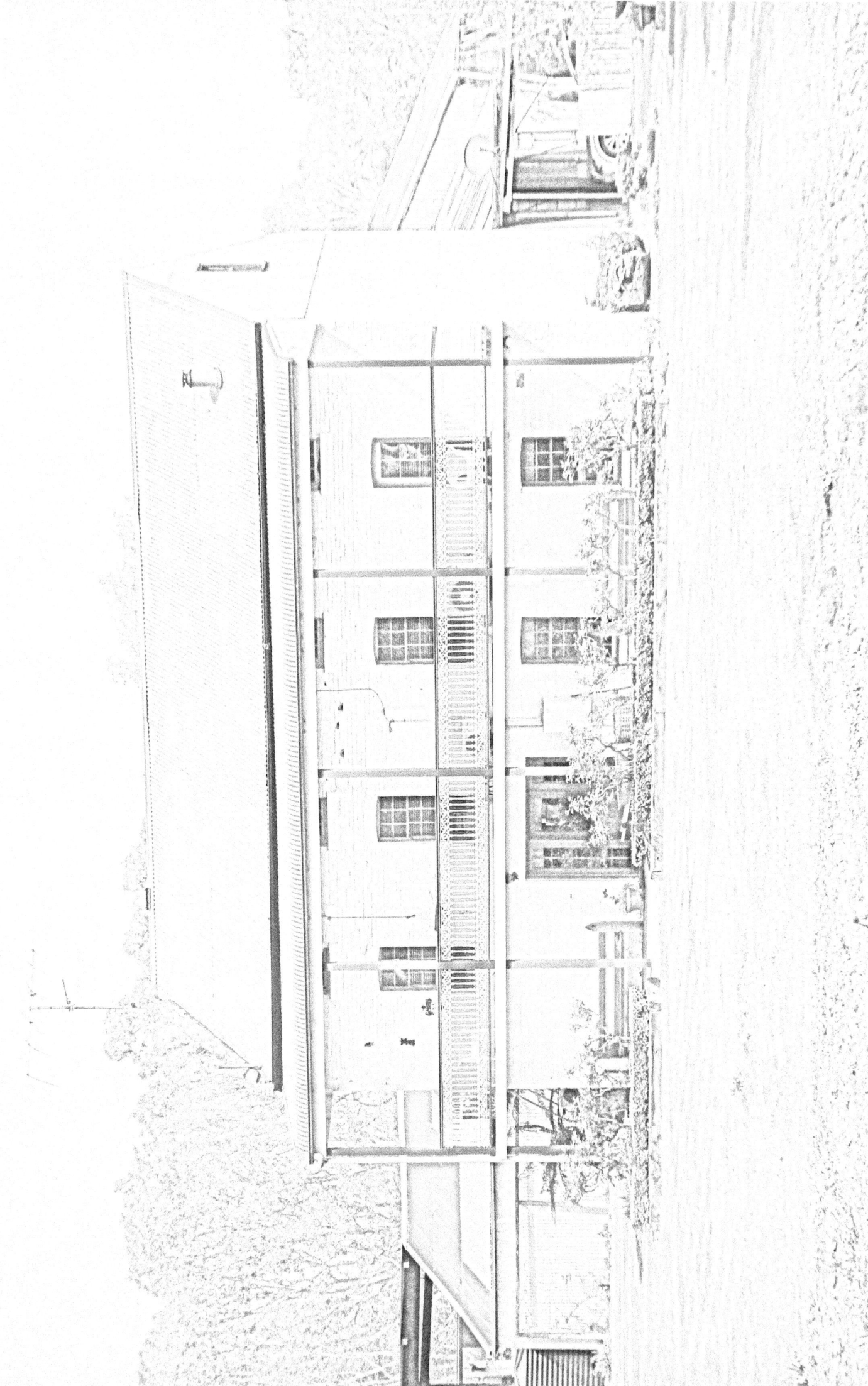

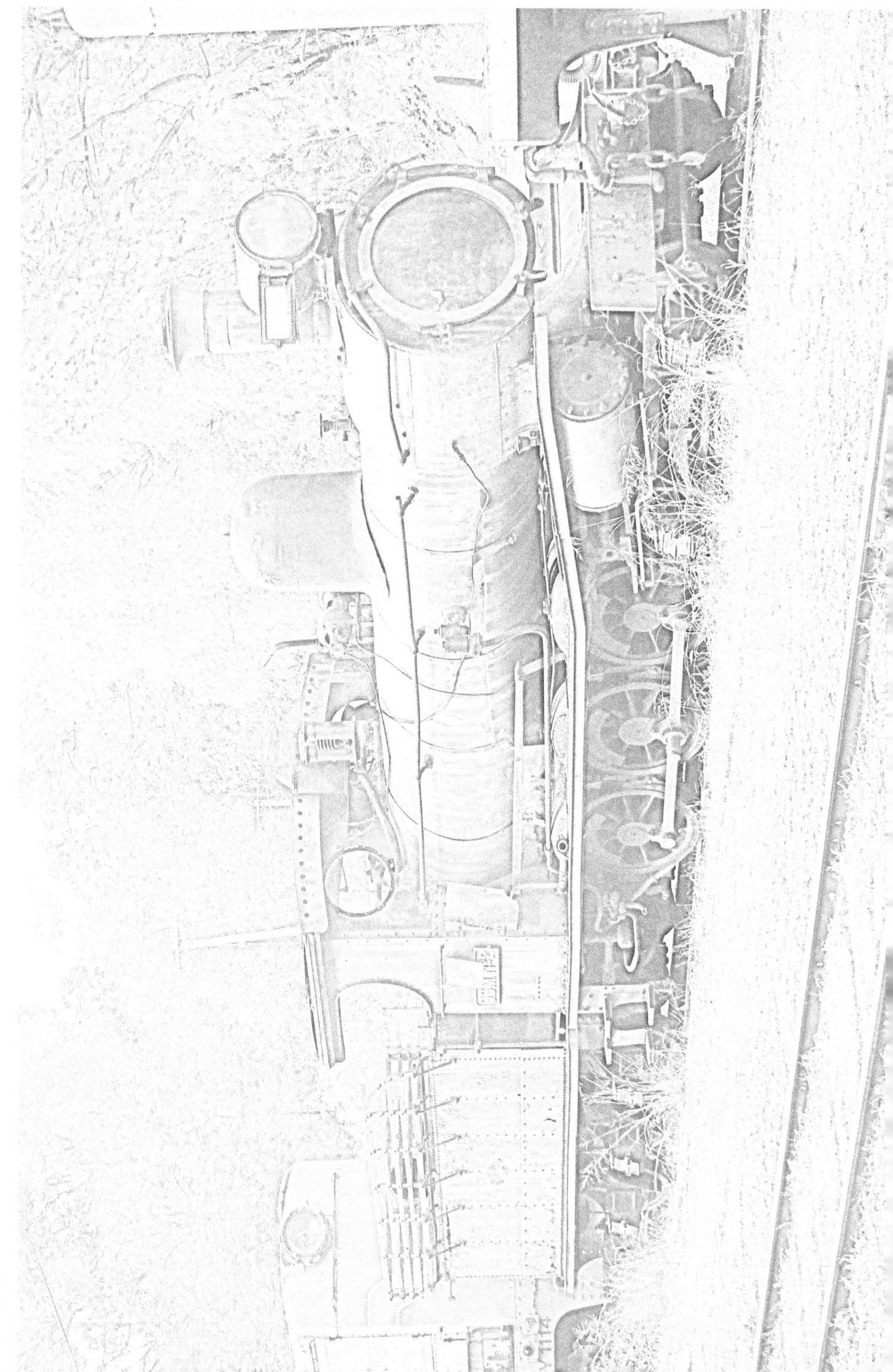

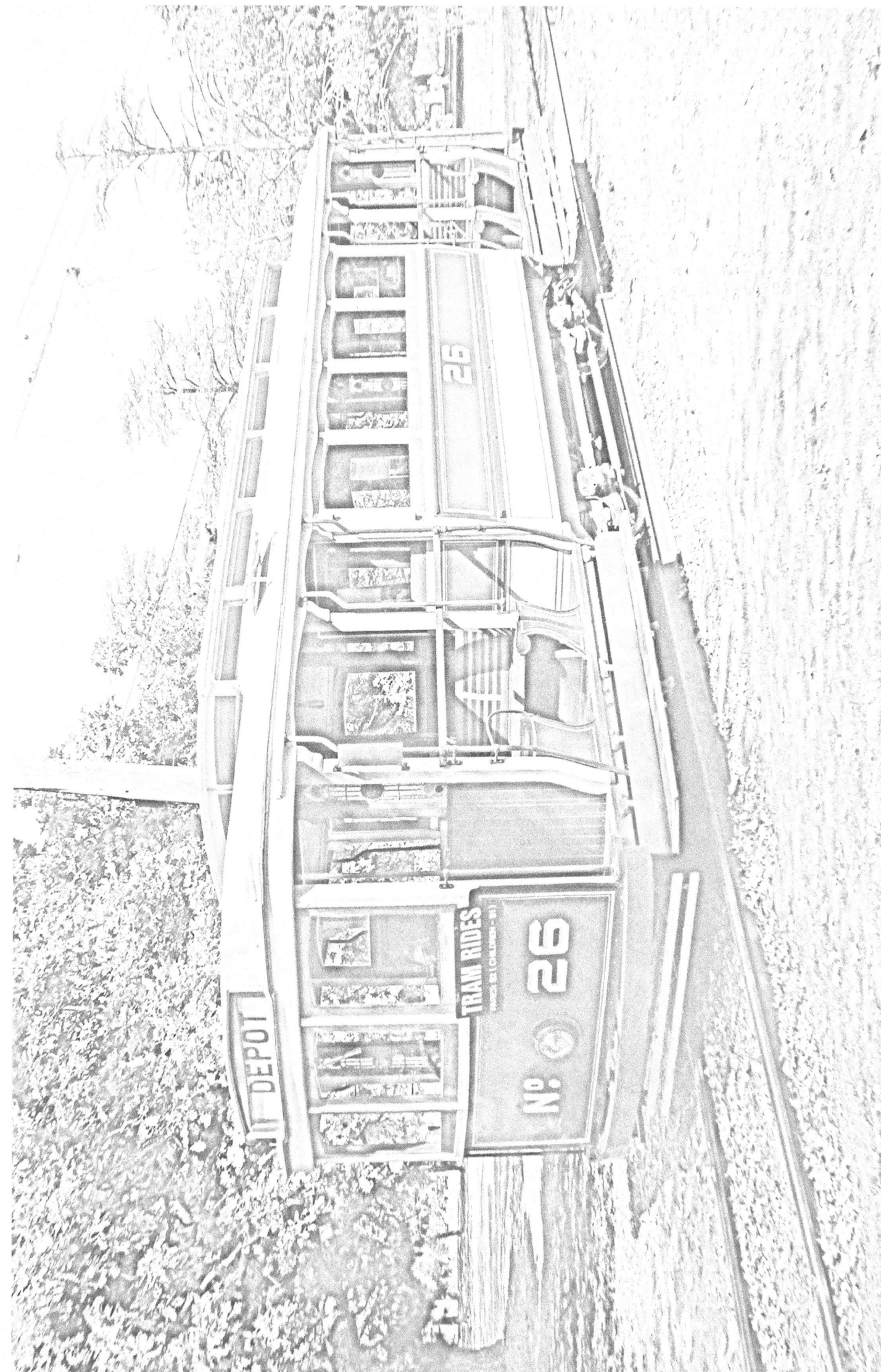

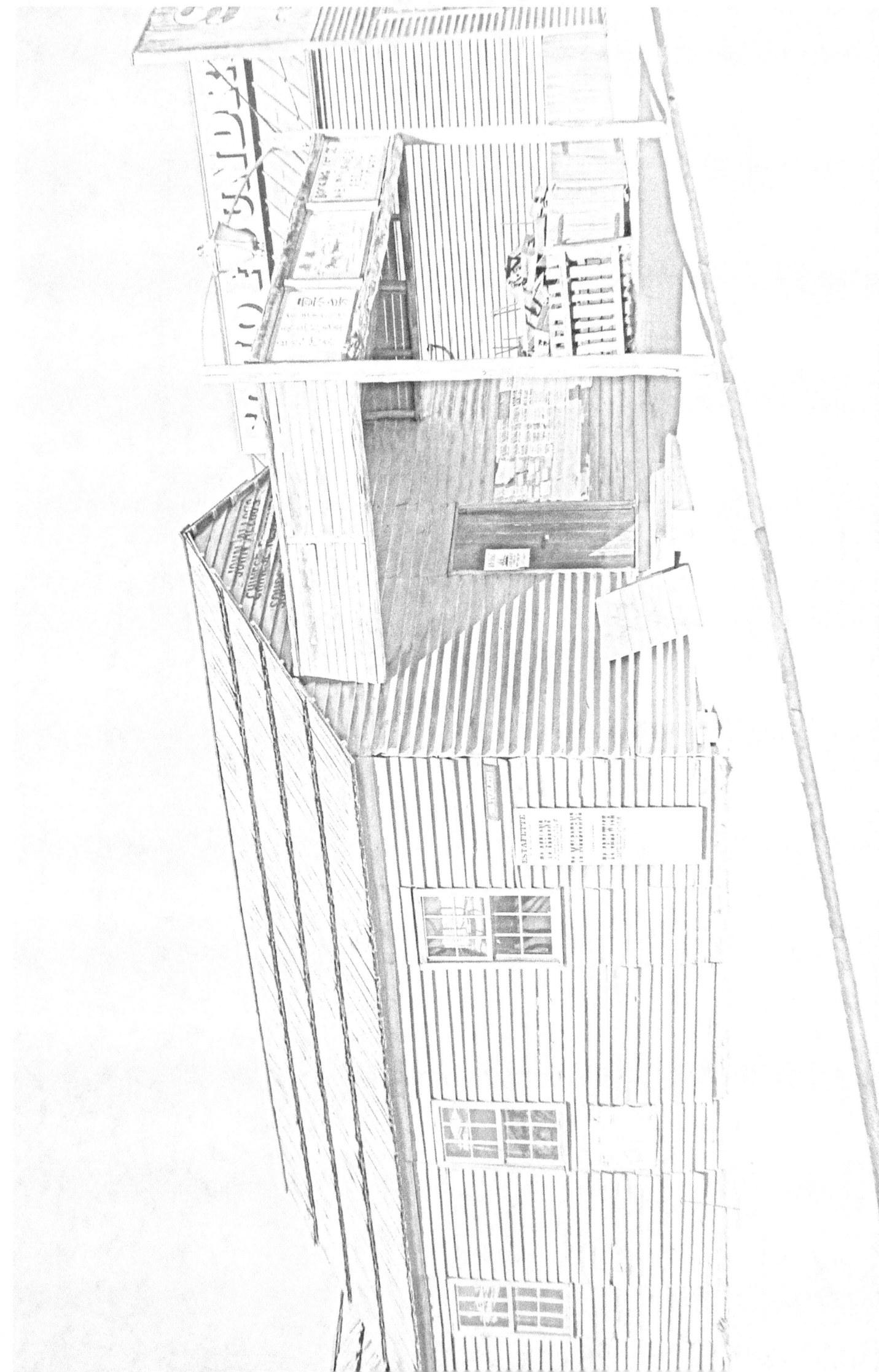

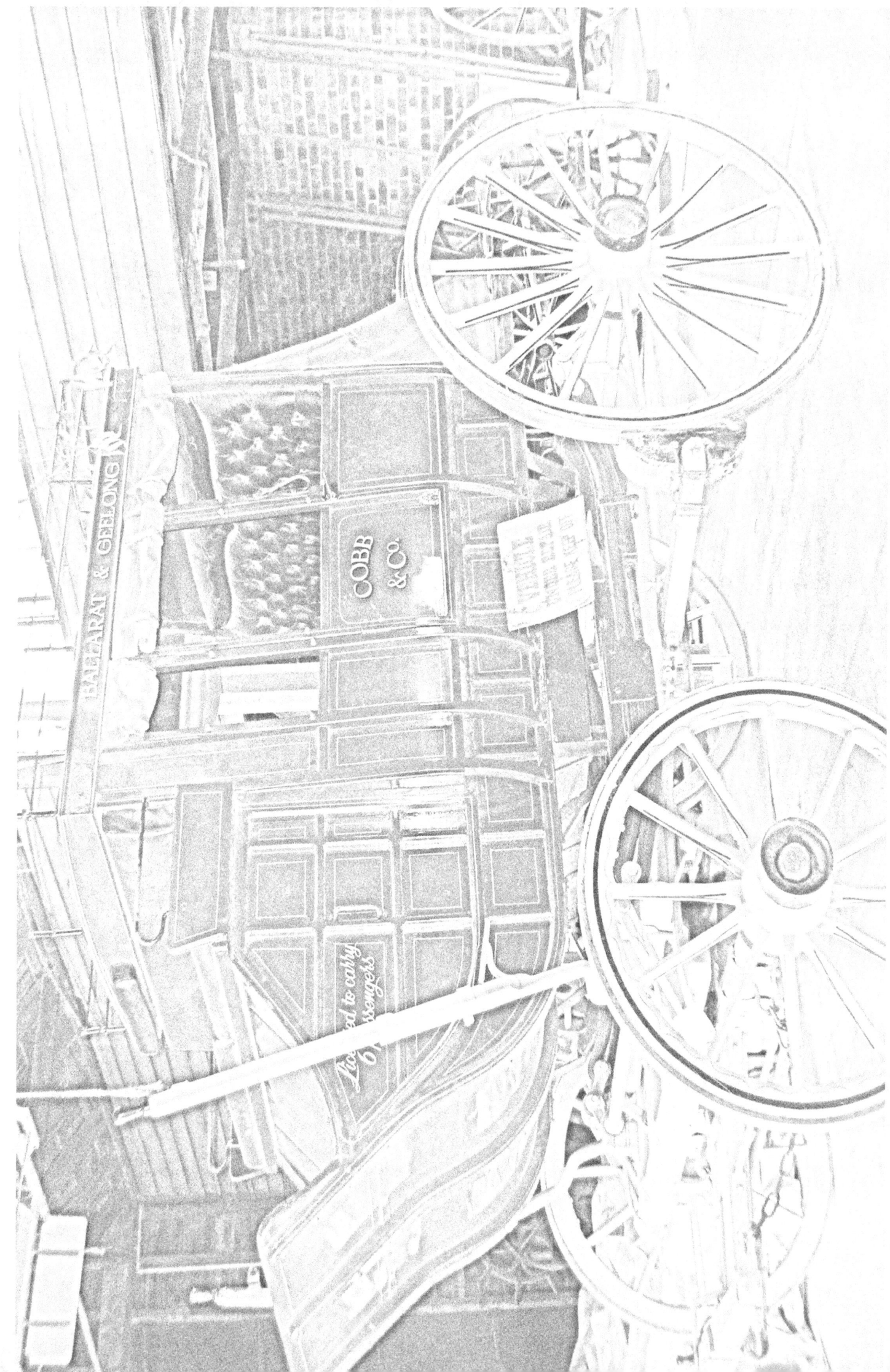

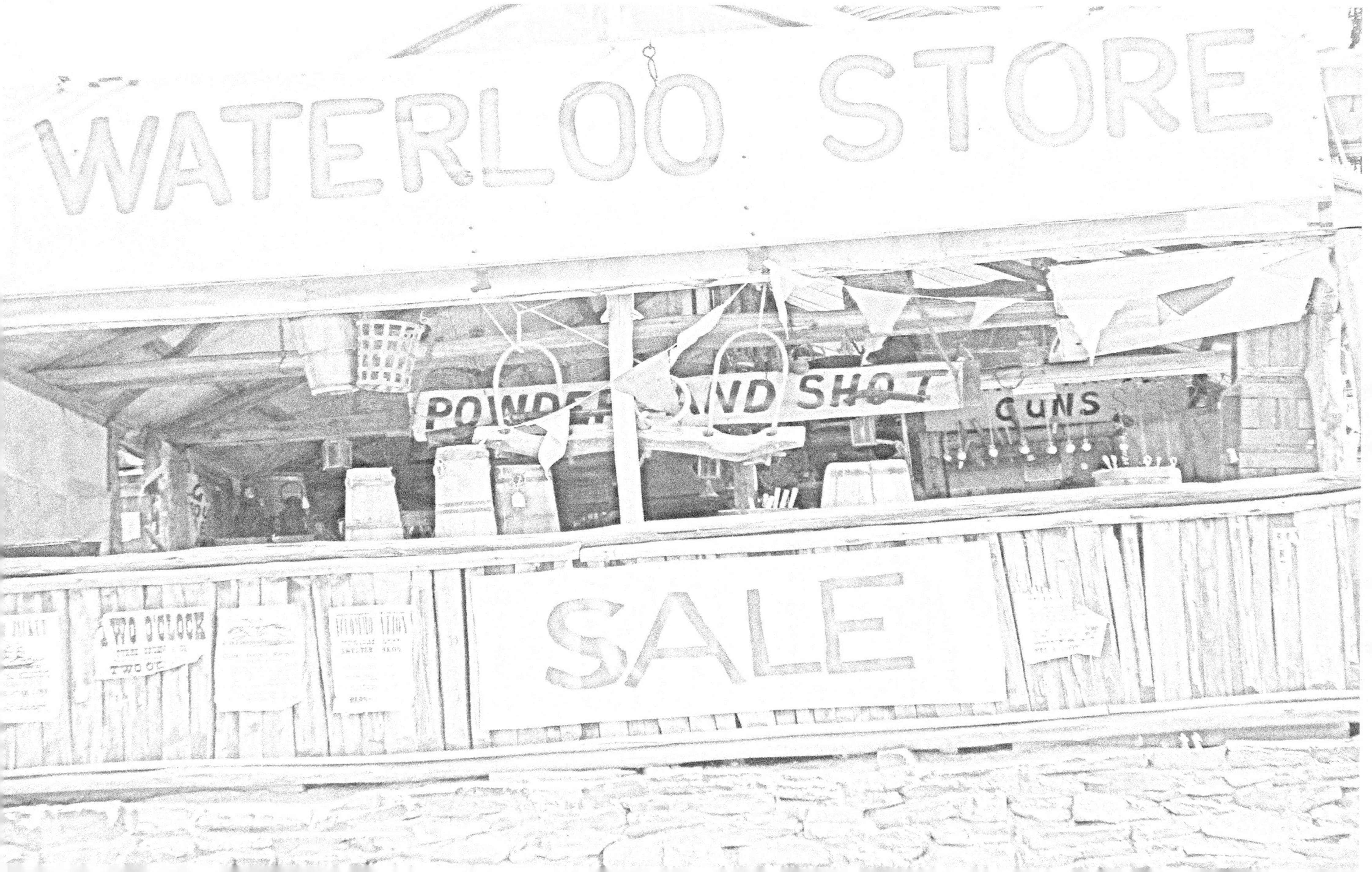
WATERLOO STORE
POWDER AND SHOT
GUNS
SALE
TWO O'CLOCK

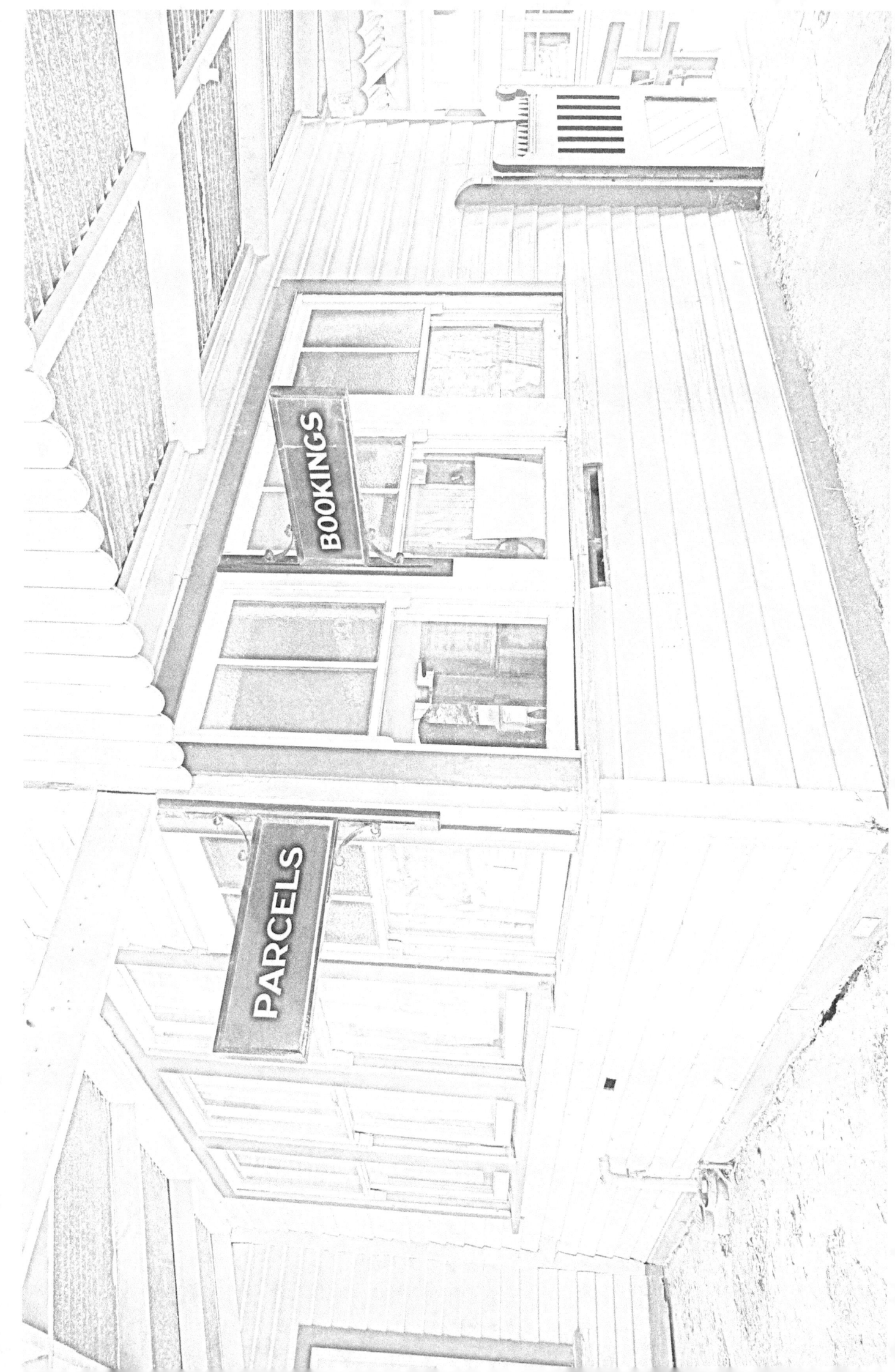

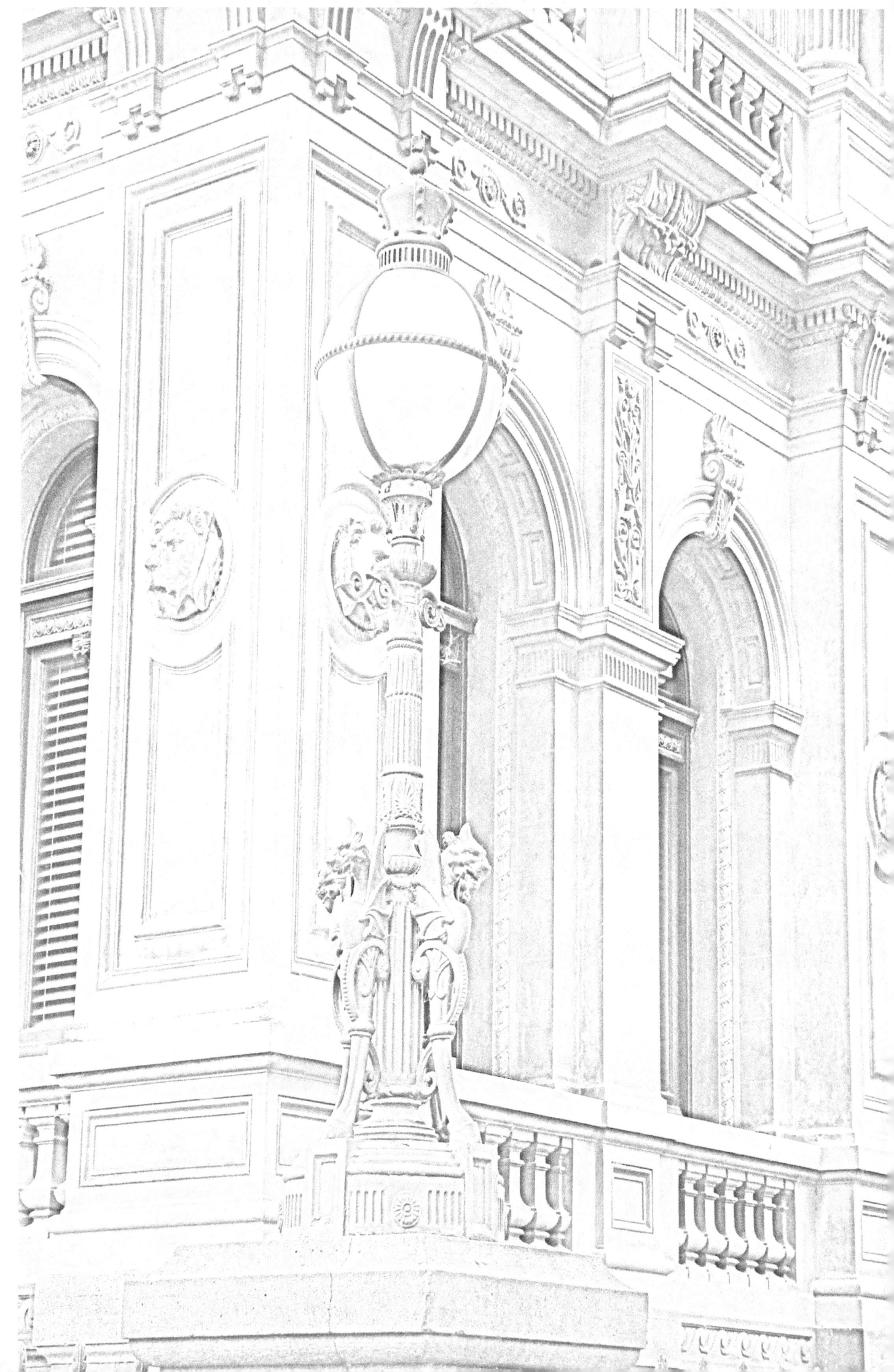

Big Strawberry

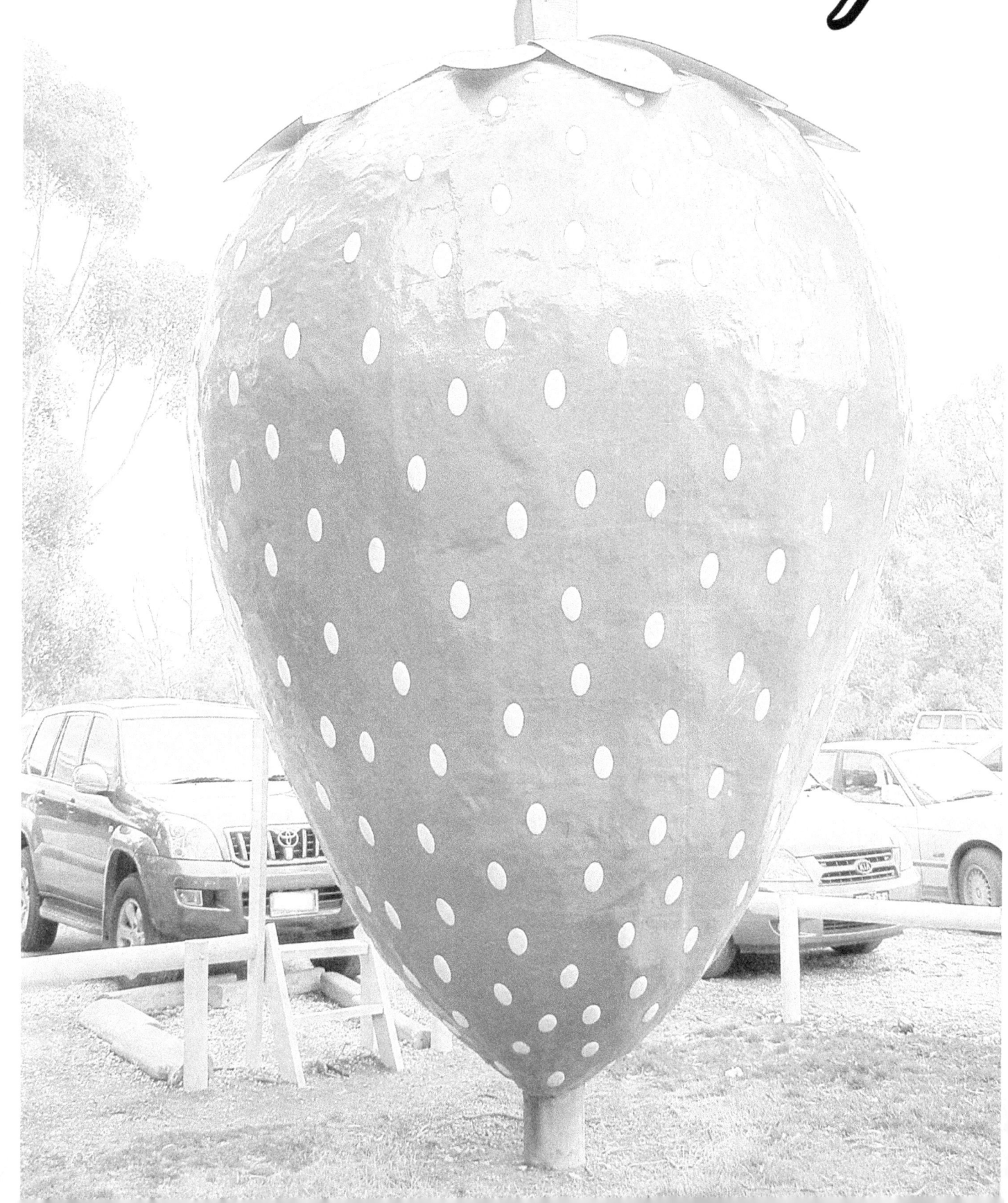

Cunnamulla Fella

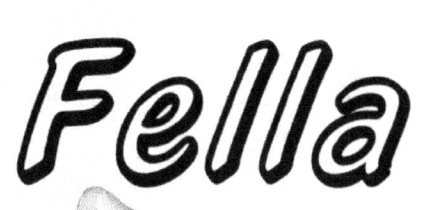

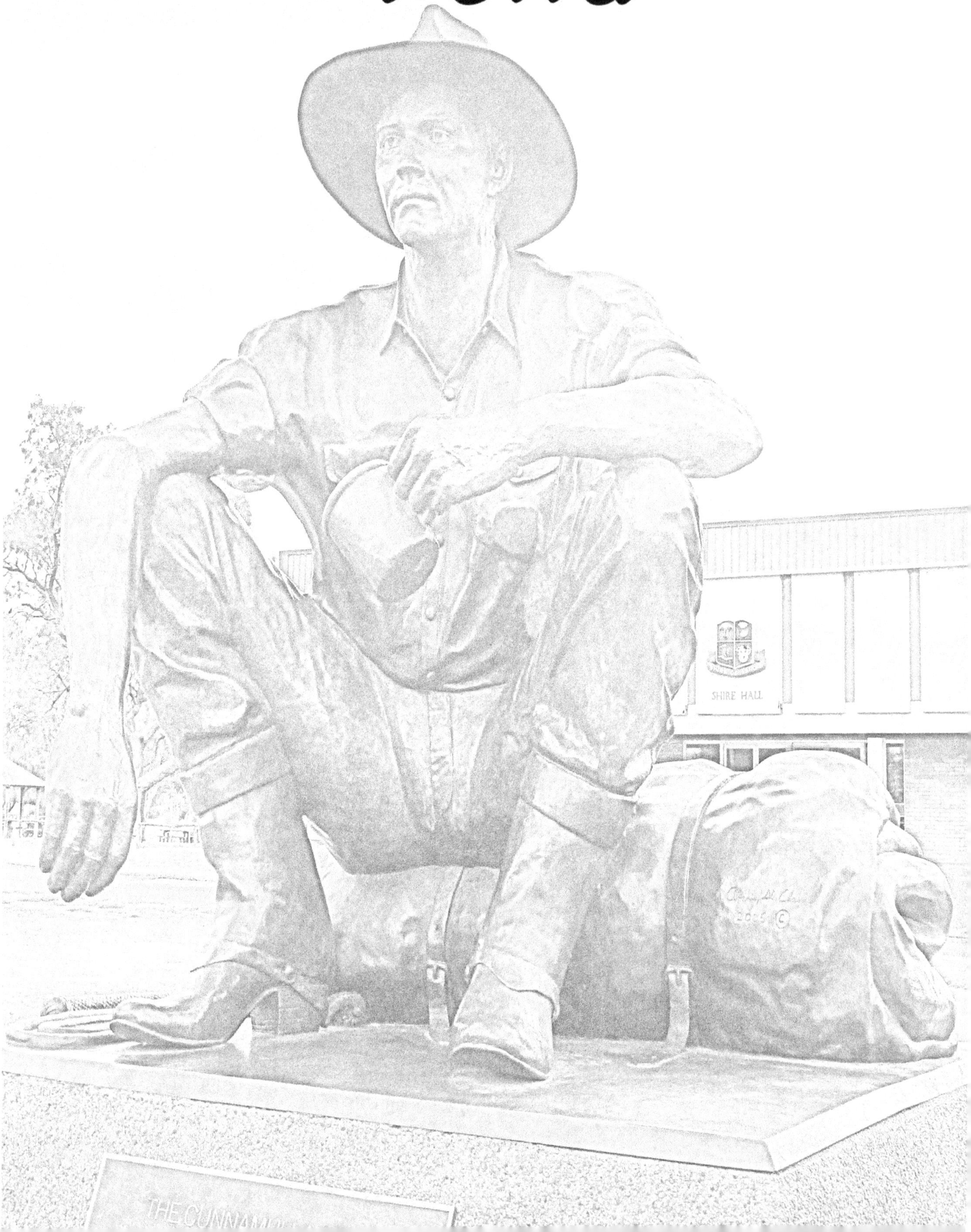

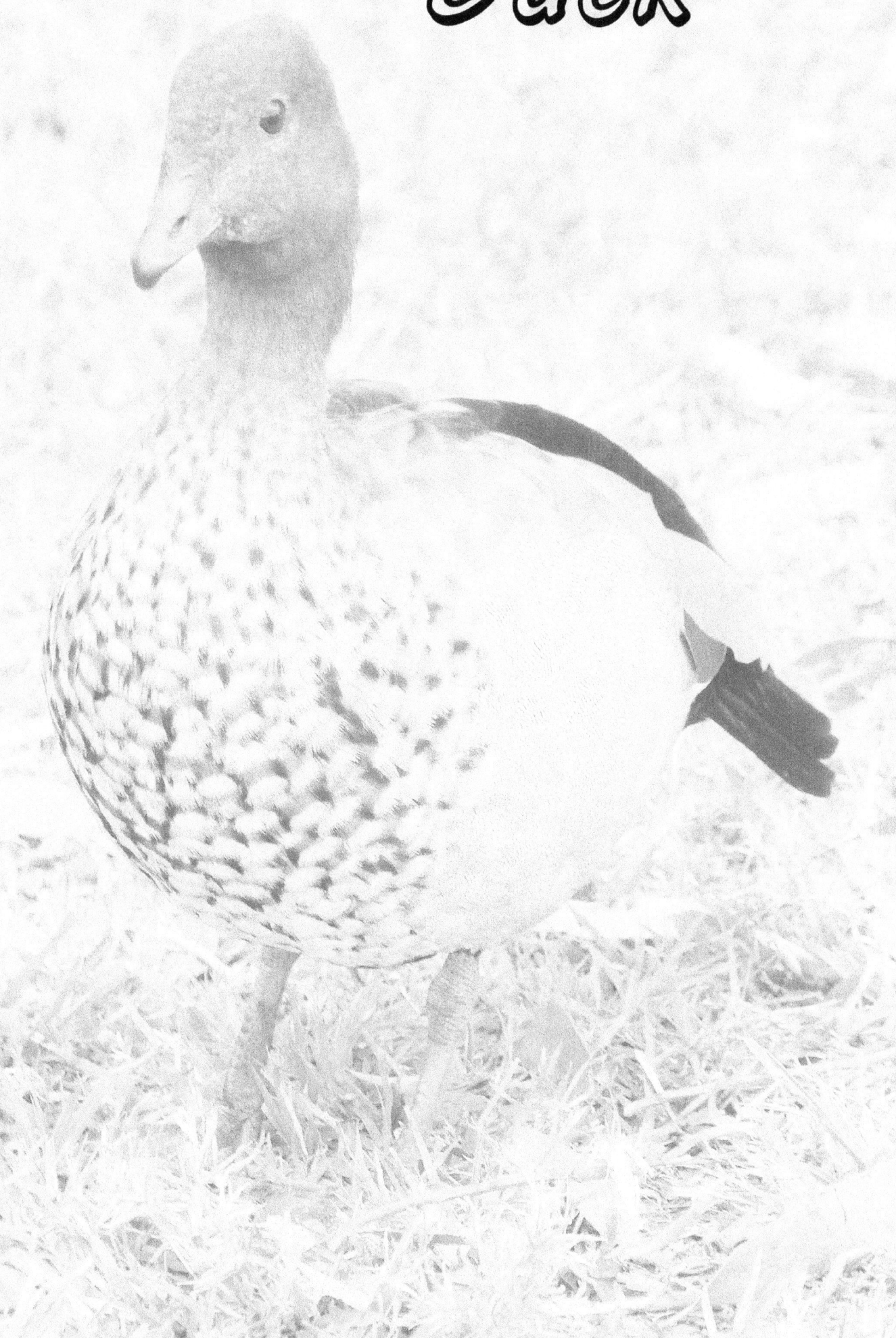

Duck

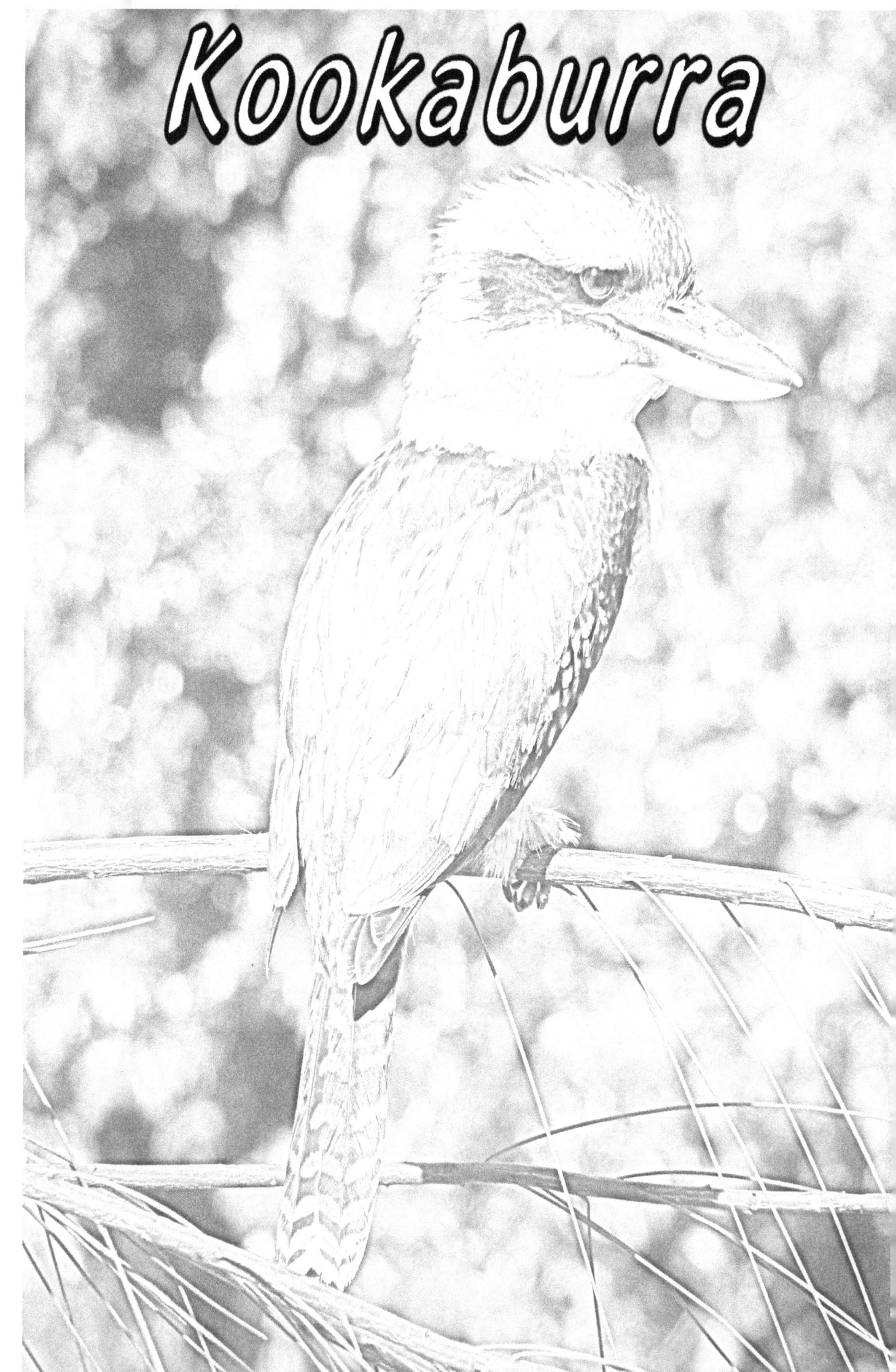

Kookaburra

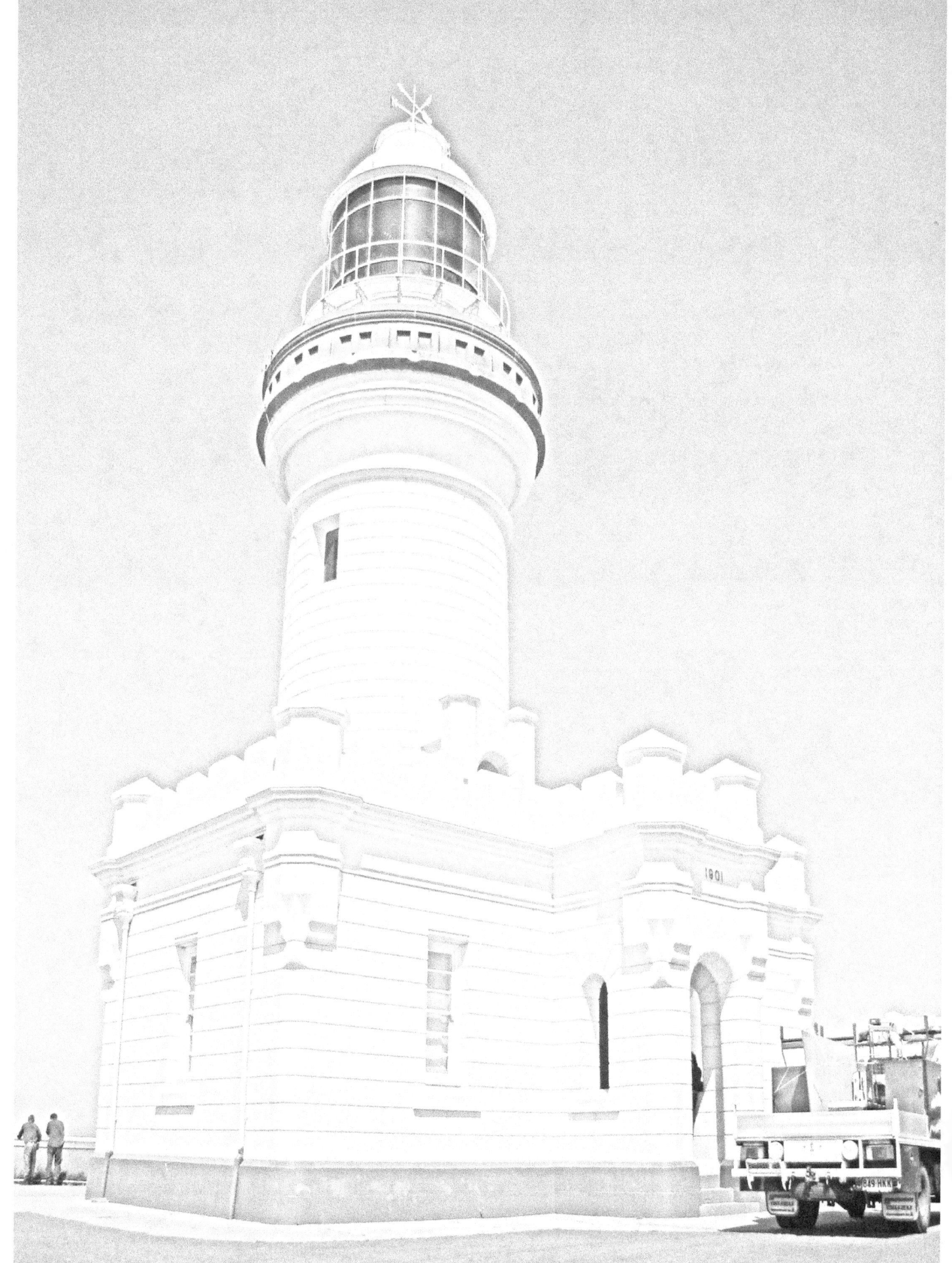

Lighthouse

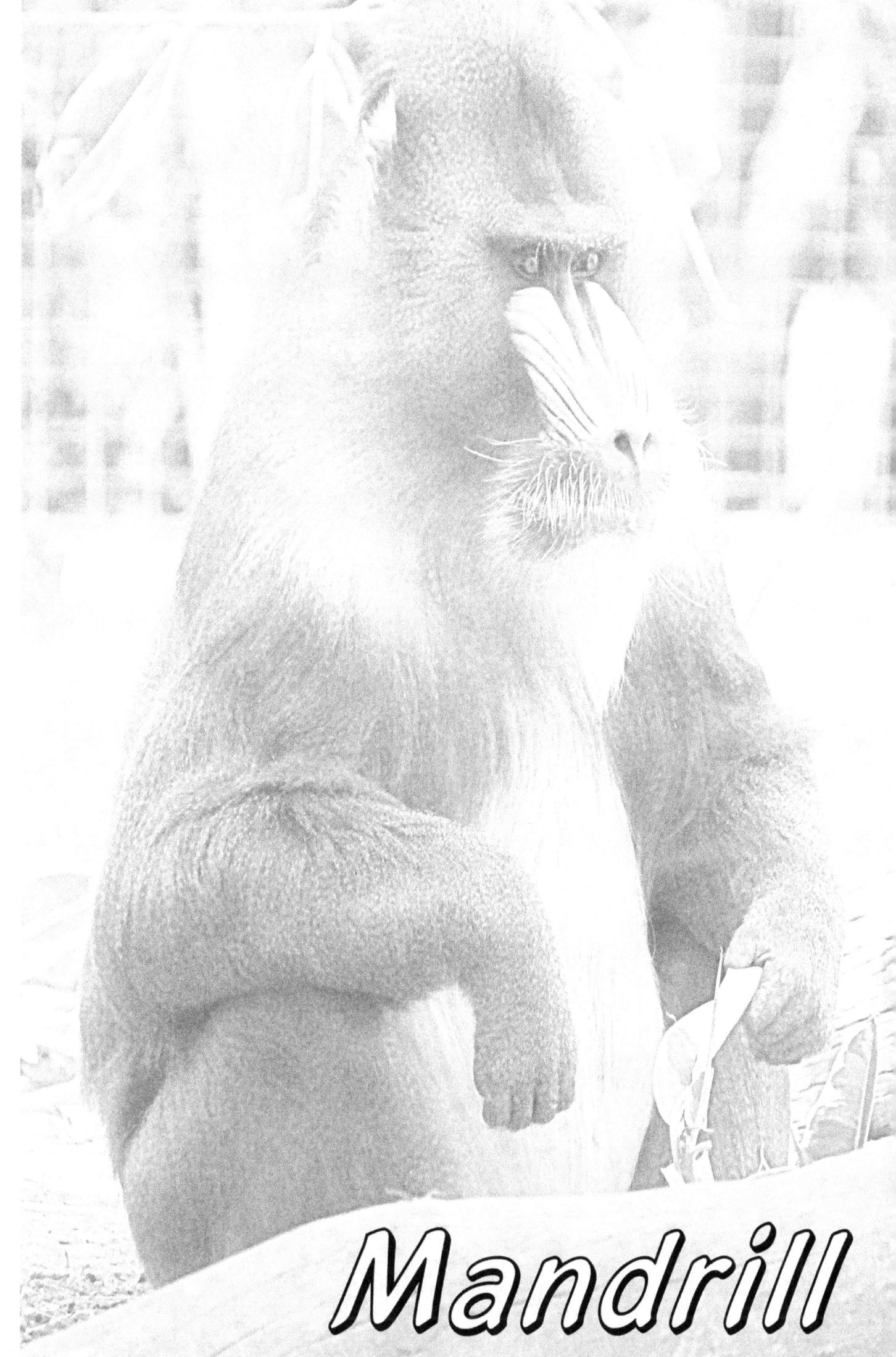

Mandrill

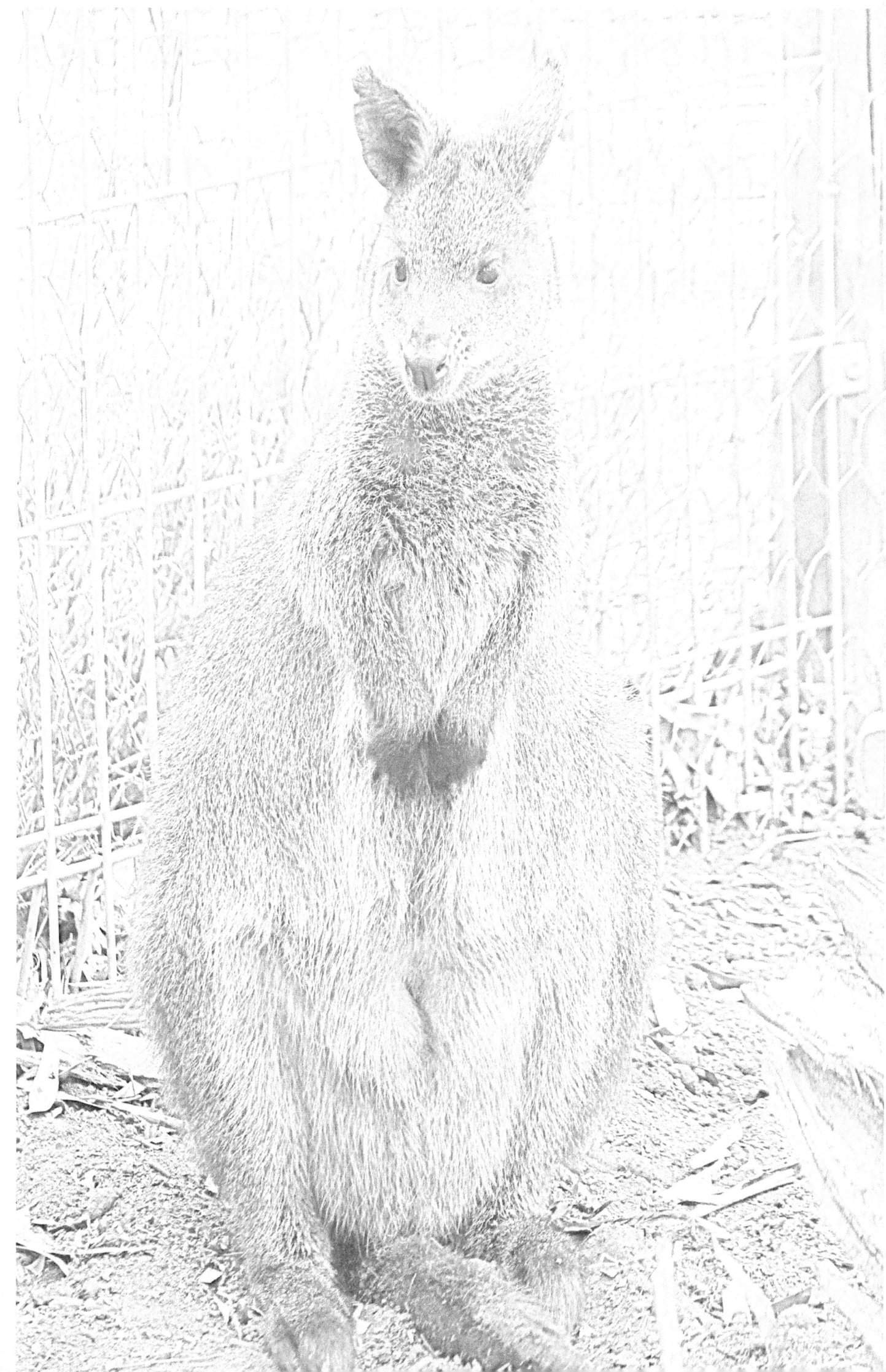

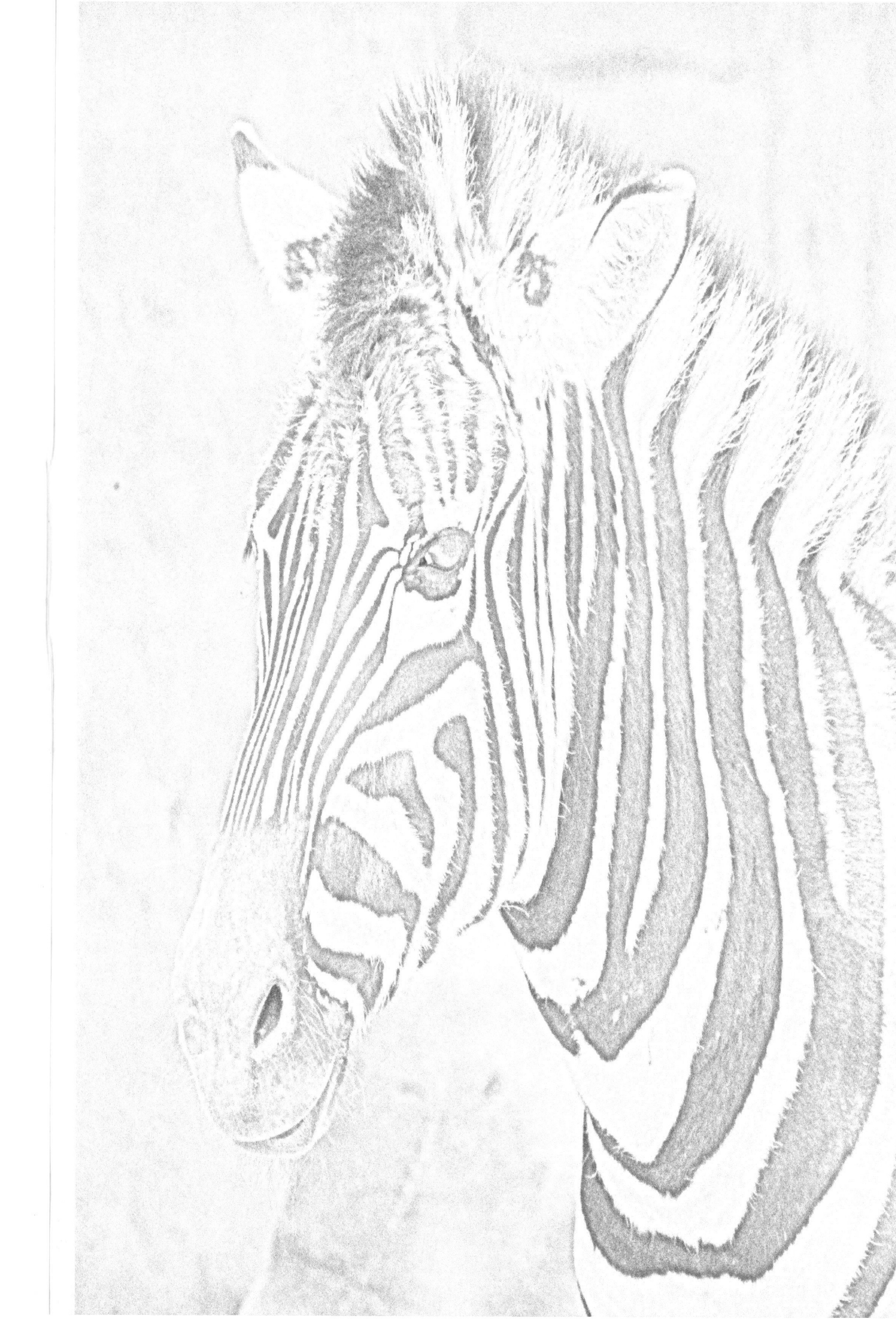

9 780359 787807